A Trainer's Guide
to
The Creative Curriculum®
for Family Child Care

Diane Trister Dodge
Laura J. Colker

TEACHING
STRATEGIES®
INC.

Washington, DC

Developed with funds received under an Innovative Head Start Grant
from the U.S. Department of Health and Human Services to the National
Child Day Care Association, Inc., Washington, DC.

Teaching Strategies, Inc.
P.O. Box 42243
Washington, DC 20015
ISBN 0-9602892-8-3
LCCN 90-071846

Printed and bound in the United States of America
Third Printing: June 2003

Acknowledgments

The development of this training guide, like the curriculum it accompanies, was truly a collaborative effort. The talents and experience of many individuals contributed to the final product. In particular, we would like to single out Kris Hansen, who was the creative spirit behind many of the workshops, and Leanne Sponsel, who enthusiastically reviewed the entire document and provided suggestions that enhanced the manual.

We are also indebted to several colleagues for developing and polishing the manuscript into finished form:

Beth Hudgins: design and layout

Julie Headland: cover design

Martha Cooley: editing and proofing

Frank Harvey and Julie Mikuta: word processing and production.

To all of these individuals, we extend our heartfelt appreciation for their assistance and support.

A Trainer's Guide to The Creative Curriculum for Family Child Care

Introduction

Family child care is a growing and important profession. Many parents who work outside their homes choose family child care for their children because of the benefits this environment offers: smaller groups of children, a calmer, home-like atmosphere, and the capacity to care for children of various ages—thus enabling the same provider to care for two or more siblings of different ages.

Family child care providers offer children and families a significant service. Children gain a secure environment where they can learn to trust other adults and children, and pursue activities that stimulate their growth and development—including the satisfactions of learning from older children, and teaching children younger than themselves. Parents, knowing that their children are safe and comfortable, can focus on workplace obligations. Parents also benefit from formal and informal interactions with the family child care provider and the other parents.

Family child care coordinators and trainers can play a central role in reaching out to providers (who might otherwise work in isolation), involving them in support networks and helping them achieve their goals. By making training and on-site assistance available, trainers can help providers offer a high-quality program.

How *The Creative Curriculum for Family Child Care* Can Help

One of the key measures of quality is the degree to which the program offered is developmentally appropriate for the children who are served. An effective strategy for achieving this type of program is to implement a high-quality curriculum. *The Creative Curriculum for Family Child Care* is a comprehensive and practical curriculum that can help both providers and trainers achieve quality in family child care.

For providers, *The Creative Curriculum for Family Child Care* offers a practical and concrete plan for guiding children's learning and development in a home environment. It illustrates how children grow and learn at each stage of development. Using child growth and development as a foundation, *The Creative Curriculum* offers easy-to-implement strategies for organizing daily experiences that meet the needs of infants, toddlers, preschoolers, and school-age children. In *The Creative Curriculum* providers will find a practical approach to planning and implementing a program that will make their role easier and more rewarding.

Trainers and family child care coordinators will find that *The Creative Curriculum* offers a central focus for the role they play in supporting providers. It can provide the content for training sessions. It can also be used as the framework for working with providers in their homes to plan and implement a developmentally appropriate program.

This *Trainer's Guide* is designed to assist trainers and family child care coordinators who wish to use *The Creative Curriculum for Family Child Care* as the focus for both workshops and on-site training. If you are an experienced trainer or coordinator of a family child care program, you know the importance of individualizing your training and supervision. No two providers learn in the same way or have the same strengths or needs. For example, some providers will be eager to read a curriculum that specifically provides guidance on programming. They may be able to implement the ideas on their own or with a minimal amount of assistance. Other providers may be overwhelmed by the size of the workbook or even the idea that they should use a curriculum to plan their program. They will need to be introduced to the value of using a curriculum and encouraged to implement it in small steps.

Content and Format of the Trainer's Guide

Two key approaches to working with providers on implementing *The Creative Curriculum for Family Child Care* are presented in this *Trainer's Guide*. The first approach involves bringing providers together periodically for workshops and sharing sessions. The second approach is the individualized support you offer in each provider's home.

Chapter I, Planning Effective Training Sessions, reviews what we know about adult learners as the basis for planning all training. It offers practical suggestions on logistics, training techniques, communicating with providers, and assessing the training.

Chapter II, Workshops on *The Creative Curriculum for Family Child Care*, includes detailed workshop outlines on each of the major activity areas in the *Curriculum*.

Chapters III and IV deal with working with providers in their homes. These chapters explain what should be happening in family child care homes where the *Creative Curriculum* is being used and why these things are important. Here you will find specific guidance on setting the stage and on each of the activities in the *Curriculum*. These chapters include some of the typical problems that providers experience and strategies for assisting providers in addressing these problems.

The Appendix includes a list of resources that can supplement the information provided in the *Creative Curriculum* and professional organizations that providers can join.

Where to Start

We expect that trainers and family child care coordinators will use this *Trainer's Guide* in a variety of ways. If you enjoy giving workshops and have established regularly scheduled training sessions for providers, you will find the workshop outlines a good place to start. Review them and decide which ones best address the needs and interests of the providers you work with. Adapt and build on the suggestions to suit your training preferences and style.

If the focus of your work with providers involves visiting them in their homes and providing support and training on-site, the chapters on working with providers in their homes will offer you a wealth of ideas on what to look for and how to individualize your support. Based on what you know of each provider, you can select from these chapters the topics that are most relevant during a particular visit and work with individual providers on these areas.

I. Planning Effective Training Sessions

One of the most effective ways to introduce providers to *The Creative Curriculum for Family Child Care* is to offer training sessions that bring providers together. Effective training depends on an understanding of how adults learn and careful attention to training strategies.

Understanding How Adults Learn

In planning training on the *Creative Curriculum*—or any subject, for that matter—it's important to reflect on what we know about how adults learn. Doing so, we can maximize our effectiveness as trainers. In teaching young children, we would never attempt, for example, to teach them pre-math concepts such as patterning or classifying without first taking into consideration how children learn. Before they can begin to classify objects by size or shape, children first need to have lots of direct experiences with table toys, blocks, and other materials so that they can identify their physical properties. Once they learn that blocks have shape and color, children can learn to sort by these characteristics. By applying learning theory, we thus facilitate learning.

The same is true for adults. Just as learning theory helps us prepare the environment and tailor the content to fit children's needs, so does it help us accomplish these same objectives with adults. Several concepts can be regarded as guiding principles of adult learning theory. They can serve as guidelines for you as you plan your training program.

- Adults bring to training a wealth of previous experiences.

- Adults perceive their own experiences as unique and private. They are not always comfortable or willing to share these experiences with a group.

- For adults, time is a valuable investment. They need to be convinced that their time will not be wasted at a training session.

- Adults are self-directed. They like to retain control of the learning experience.

- Adults learn in a variety of ways and styles; however, methods in which the adult learner actively participates—in addition to watching and listening—are preferred by the majority of adults.

- Motivation for learning is closely related to the perceived immediate utility of the information being taught.

In applying these tenets of adult education to your training program, consider using these techniques:[1]

- **Share the specific training goals and objectives with participants.** Effective training involves developing a shared group commitment to goals and objectives.

- **Draw on participants' experiences.** Training becomes more meaningful when participants can relate concepts to personal situations and experiences.

- **Establish from the beginning that participants are responsible for their own learning.** It is important to state at the outset that everyone will take something different from the session, depending on what is important to them, how much effort they put into the session, and whether they integrate and use what they learn.

- **Emphasize the development of skills rather than the rote learning of responses.** Learning is the process of assimilating new information and using it to improve skills.

- **Encourage trainees' active involvement.** Role playing, small group analysis, discussion, and case studies afford participants the opportunity to apply training concepts, principles, and strategies to real-life situations.

- **Allow trainees to make interpretations and draw conclusions.** Trainers should provide the background information, data, and examples needed to permit the group to identify patterns or trends, to make generalizations, and to draw conclusions on their own.

- **Plan a balance of different types of activities using a variety of instructional media.** A balance of approaches contributes to the group's interest and ultimately ensures greater retention and application of skills and content.

Further information on applying the principles of adult learning theory to training situations will be discussed later in this chapter in the section on training techniques.

Logistics

No matter what the topic, training is most successful when it is well planned. What may seem like simple details can enhance or destroy a workshop. Attention to logistics is worth the time you will need to invest up front. Here are some general pointers that will help you ensure everyone's comfort:

- Schedule training sessions at times that will be most convenient for providers—for example, on Saturday mornings or, if applicable, on pre-arranged "in-service" days. Providers have steady demands on their time, both professionally and

---

[1]Based on *A Guide for Education Coordinators in Head Start*, U.S. Department of Health and Human Services, Washington, DC, 1986, pp. 169-170.

personally. By accommodating their schedules, you are not just being courteous; you are also maximizing the possibilities of high attendance.

- Arrange for babysitting on-site where training is to be held. Since many providers have small children of their own, by advertising the availability of this service, you automatically eliminate a possible obstacle to attendance at the training session.

- Provide snacks for both trainees and the children being cared for. By letting participants know in advance that food and drink are available, you eliminate another deterrent to attendance. A snack break will also refresh minds and energize participants.

- Make sure that all materials and equipment needed for training have been arranged for or prepared in advance. This includes audiovisual equipment, films, flip charts, markers, tape, chalk, handouts, and evaluation sheets. Ensure that all equipment is in working order with the necessary replacement bulbs, extension cords, and adapters on hand.

- Check that the training room is comfortable prior to the start of training. Chairs need to be roomy enough for participants to sit for a long period of time without getting restless. Participants will also need something to write on (other than their laps). The room temperature should be appropriate, and air should be circulating freely. An overheated room can put an audience to sleep more quickly than a boring speaker.

- Arrange furniture in a pattern that suits your working style. Most trainers prefer circles, semi-circles, or small groupings of tables. As a general rule, training is best received when the room is informally arranged.

- Display name tags, sign-in sheets, agendas, and reference materials in areas that are readily accessible to participants.

- Arrange for you or someone associated with the training to greet participants when they enter the training room. By individually welcoming providers, you'll set them at ease.

- At the outset, let participants know the rules that will be in effect. If, for example, a "no smoking" rule is imposed, participants should be advised about areas where smoking is permitted during breaks.

- Before beginning, point out the location of rest rooms, telephones, and water fountains. This will cut down on interruptions once training starts.

By attending to these few logistical concerns, you'll find that the content of the training program itself will be the focus of your attention—not scramblings for extension cords or searches for engineers to turn up the heat. Preparation goes a long way when it comes to training.

Introducing Training to Providers

For some providers, training will be a new experience. Even an experienced provider may feel shy about talking aloud in a group, sharing experiences and ideas, or asking questions. As a trainer, one of your most important functions is to help participants feel comfortable about expressing their views. Here are some ideas you might try to help providers feel more comfortable during training:

- Acknowledge that sharing ideas and experiences in a group may feel a little uncomfortable at first.

- Underscore the importance of training for the provider. Stress that the sole purpose of training is to help providers do their jobs better.

- Encourage providers to express their opinions. Emphasize that everyone's views are valuable and that there is usually more than one "right" way to approach a topic.

- Look for visual "body-language" cues that will alert you to the fact that someone may be uncomfortable with the subject matter being discussed (squirming), shy about contributing (eye avoidance), or angry (turning away with the entire body). Then try to respond to what you see.

- Ask questions appropriately in response to cues you receive from the audience. At times, both direct questions ("What books do you think would be helpful to a child whose parents are divorcing?") and open-ended questions ("How would you handle that situation?") are needed. Also, refer a question to the entire group if you sense that an in-depth discussion would be beneficial. ("That's a tough problem. Does anyone have a suggestion?")

- Don't embarrass participants by forcing each person to contribute.

- If conflicts or disagreements occur, guide the discussion to encourage compromise or at least acceptance of conflicting points of view.

- Use small group activities as opportunities to discuss feelings, either through role playing, simulations, or problem-solving assignments.

- Encourage participants to be active listeners as well as active discussants.

- Make yourself available to discuss issues and topics with participants during breaks. Some providers may be more comfortable sharing their views with you on a one-on-one basis rather than in front of the whole group.

Training Techniques

To a large extent your choice of training techniques will depend on your personal preferences and philosophy of training. For example, if you're a skilled lecturer, you will enjoy including mini-lectures as part of your workshops. On the other hand, if you're uncomfortable as a lecturer, you should feel free to rely on group-oriented activities. Your choice of techniques should also include an understanding of the preferences of those whom you are training. This means that you should select techniques that suit your style but be aware of the fact that in order to meet the different learning styles of the people you'll be training, you'll have to use a variety of approaches and methods.

The training techniques listed here represent a potpourri of ideas. Some of these techniques will be perfect for you; others will not. Try out as many techniques as possible to find those that suit you. You'll find that nearly all these techniques can be modified and reshaped to accommodate both your needs and the needs of the groups you'll be training.

Written Handouts

Written material such as articles from professional journals or chapters in textbooks can be used as background reading or to provide further illustration of topics only touched on during training. You might wish to use written materials as summaries of presented content, as training assignments, or as supplemental readings for interested participants.

Audiovisuals

Audiovisuals can be very effective training tools. For example, the videotape *Caring and Learning* shows realistic and relevant scenes that can help providers visualize how to implement the ideas presented in a workshop. Slides you take of family child care homes would also be a good way to share some of the ideas you uncover in your home visits. Showing slides allows you to reinforce good practices and enables providers to learn more about each other.

Overheads

Overhead transparencies are recommended as accompaniments to presentations. They not only break up the monotony of the spoken voice but also reinforce for participants the key points of a lecture. Here are some suggestions for developing transparencies:

- Include key words and phrases only.

- Use large printed letters so that the overhead can be read from any point in the room.

- Keep color to a minimum and only to highlight, not decorate.

- Be sure that the contrast between the background color and lettering is sufficient for easy reading.

- Keep illustrations (if any) simple.

- Graphs, if used, should be simple and readily understood.

Problem-Solving Activities

One of the most popular—and effective—training techniques is group problem-solving. Brainstorming solutions to realistic problems energizes a group and generates lots of creative ideas. The theory behind brainstorming is to separate idea creation from idea evaluation. It works best in groups of 5 to 12; a recorder and a moderator are needed. Here are the rules for brainstorming:

- All ideas are listed; no critical remarks are allowed.

- "Hitchhiking" is permissible—if one participant can improve upon or combine previously mentioned ideas, so much the better.

- "Freewheeling" is encouraged—even outlandish ideas keep the group momentum going.

- The more the better—the more ideas generated, the more likely there will be some viable solutions among these ideas.

- Evaluation comes only after all ideas have been generated.

To illustrate how this technique works, consider asking participants to brainstorm on any of the following topics:

- how they could furnish their home with toys using household objects and no more than $25 in cash;

- ways to involve parents in the child care program;

- fundraising efforts to increase resources for the family child care home; and

- community resources that should be consulted regularly.

Some other problem-solving techniques you might wish to try using include these:

- **Reverse brainstorming,** in which participants identify all the negative aspects of a problem that need to be remedied. This can be especially useful in examining practices to see what isn't working, such as why children are getting into fights during the day.

- The **slip method**, in which participants write their solutions to a stated problem on slips of paper that are collected and grouped into logical categories for analysis and discussion. This can be especially useful in coming up with plausible solutions to a specific problem, such as how to get parents to pick up their children on time.

- The **Delphi technique (group approach),** in which individual participants generate as many responses to a particular problem as they can. Ideas are then consolidated and presented for the group to consider and rank in order of viability. Through this filtering process, 3 to 5 "best" solutions to particular problems can be identified.

Case Studies

The chief advantage of the case study method is that it helps participants apply what has been taught through lectures or assigned reading to real-life examples. By providing an illustrative story, case studies can be a powerful tool for helping participants apply theory to the real world. Here is a sample case study that might be used in conjunction with a workshop on sand and water play.

Sample Case Study

Provider X has three children in her care: a 13-month-old mobile infant, a 3-year-old toddler, and a 4-year-old preschooler. Her own sixth-grade daughter joins the family child care program at 3:30 p.m.

Provider X thinks it's important to include outdoor sand and water play in her program at least once a week. However, the last 10 days have been bitterly cold, and the children have not been outside long enough to organize sand and water activities.

Responding to this situation, Provider X has scheduled indoor sand and water play for today's late-morning group activity. The 4-year-old has been set up at the kitchen sink for water play, using a step stool. The 3-year-old is using a sand tub at the kitchen table. Provider X has taken the trouble to lay down protective newspapers. Each child has funnels, sieves, and measuring cups for play props.

Having just changed the baby and brought him into the kitchen, Provider X decides that it would be nice to let the infant have some sand experiences, too. She moves the child's booster chair over to the sand tub and lets the infant join in.

Almost immediately, the infant smashes the molded sand pile that the 3-year-old has just finished forming. This upsets the older child, and he swats the baby. The infant starts crying; the older child returns to his sand play.

The preschooler at the sink feels compelled to see what is happening. In so doing, she drips water into the sand tub. This now causes the toddler to join the infant in screaming.

Provider X decides the only thing she can do at this point is to calm the children down, which she manages to do. As she is comforting the children, she hastily puts the sand tub on the counter and drains the sink. She diverts the children to the comfort of the living room. Sand and water play is over for today.

After reading the case, discuss the following questions:

- What went wrong?

- What might the provider have done to avoid these problems?

- Were there scheduling problems? Organizational problems?

- Should she have done something different in terms of supervision?

- Is it possible to schedule sand and water play indoors?

- What things did this provider do well?

- What suggestions/advice would you give Provider X?

Role Playing

Putting oneself in another's shoes is one of the most popular of all training techniques. It allows participants to "act out" real-life situations in a risk-free environment. By seeing things from another's perspective, participants gain insight into how better to approach a problem issue.

You might consider using role playing to have participants react to scheduling concerns, interactions with parents, or actual family child care scenarios. For example, you might have the trainees pretend they are on a field trip to the library and assign these roles:

Family child care provider	Shy toddler
Fussy infant	Children's librarian trying to enforce order
Curious toddler	Reader trying to concentrate
Chatty preschooler	Helpful parent

Through its "acting" the group could uncover procedures for getting the most from the library visit without disrupting the needs of others.

Discussion Techniques: The Fishbowl, Fantasy, and Visualization

These techniques are used by trainers to stimulate discussion. In the fishbowl technique participants are divided into two groups, forming an inner and an outer ring. Participants in the inner group are given an assignment based on content presented either through a lecture or reading. For example, you might ask the inner group how providers can use a curriculum such as the *Creative Curriculum* to enhance their professional image. While the inner group discusses this question aloud for 5 to 10 minutes, the outer group is asked to act as observers. At the end of the allotted time, the two groups switch roles. At the conclusion of the second discussion, both groups are asked to comment on what they've observed. Quite often, the discussion quickly becomes analytical because of mutual observations. This technique also stimulates discussion among participants who are initially shy about contributing.

Fantasy and visualization are techniques used to draw on participants' "right brain" (creative thinking) powers. Fantasy techniques most commonly involve asking participants to reflect on "what if…" situations—for example: "What if you had unlimited financial resources. How would you equip your family child care home?" This type of exercise allows participants to come up with the components of an ideal inventory. They can then compare the ideal to reality and see where compromises are appropriate.

Conversely, fantasy can also be used to think through worst-case scenarios. For instance, you might ask participants to reflect on this scenario:

> *Suppose you firmly believe that art should reflect children's thoughts and feelings—not those of adults. Billy Z's parents let you know they are distressed because they never have any nice coloring book drawings or models to display around their home. You try talking to the Zs about your philosophy, but it seems to fall on deaf ears. When Mrs. Z makes another critical remark, you share with her an article in* **Young Children** *that clearly spells out your point of view: that dittos and teacher-made models stifle children's creativity. Mrs. Z doesn't mention the article to you, so after 3 or 4 days you ask her if she or Mr. Z have any reaction to the article. She murmurs, "It was probably written by some teacher who couldn't draw and was afraid the kids would do better than she could." What should you do now?*

Visualization is a technique sometimes used by trainers to help participants relate the tasks at hand to experiences they've had in the past. For example, you might ask participants to think about an experience they've had in which they were forced to do something they weren't comfortable with. What were the circumstances? How did they feel? What did they do to relieve their discomfort? Did they ever get over being uncomfortable? This type of reflection might be brought in if you sense that participants are uncomfortable dealing with particular situations, such as having to communicate unpopular information to parents.

Follow-Up

Follow-up is an important part of the training process; it allows you to determine if the content presented during training is being used. Here are some thoughts on this subject:

- **Lead a "closure" exercise at the end of the training session.** Ask participants to brainstorm, as a group, how they will implement in their family child care programs what they have learned during training.

- **Provide a training-related assignment for the participants to do with you over the next few weeks.** Develop a self-evaluation form that providers can use on their own which will allow them to assess how effectively they've been able to incorporate training ideas into their programs. Providers should be encouraged to discuss the results with you.

- **Plan to spend time observing participants in their family child care homes.** By doing this you can get a good feel for how effective the training has been. Discuss what you see with the providers and, as appropriate, give them further guidance on additional resources.

- **Plan follow-up training.** At a later date, bring participants together for a meeting in which they can share what they've learned, the progress they've made, and the challenges they've met. Take this opportunity to offer more detailed information or resources that will be beneficial to the providers.

Assessing the Training

As a trainer you need to know how effectively you've met your training goals. Did the providers' understanding of the content increase? Do providers feel capable of implementing *The Creative Curriculum for Family Child Care* ? Did they feel that the training session was beneficial to them? Did they gain skills or change attitudes?

To answer these questions, you'll find that some sort of evaluation of the training program is useful. If participants are not being well served, you'll want to adjust your training as rapidly as possible to accommodate the pinpointed weaknesses.

In addition to these basic questions, it's also helpful to know which individual parts of the training program were well received. For instance, did the providers like group exercises but dislike the mini-lectures? Did they feel that too much content was presented in too short a time?

To find out how successful your training program has been, it's always helpful to administer a short (1- or 2- page) questionnaire. With the feedback from the questionnaire, you can get a feel for these issues:

- how effectively the training accomplished its stated goals;

- how valuable the training was to the participants;

- what changes to the training program are indicated; and

- whether participants will need follow-up training.

As you assess the results, though, bear in mind that not everyone is always going to be satisfied with training. Some variations in answers are to be expected, and you should revise your training program with this in mind.

The sample evaluation form that follows can be altered easily to reflect your training program. Whether you adapt this questionnaire or develop one of your own, the information you obtain will enable you to reflect on the training program once it's completed to see what elements should be maintained and what strategies might possibly be improved in future training sessions. Training assessments are a valuable tool for ensuring that your training is addressing participants' needs. Evaluation can help you be a trainer who truly serves family child care providers.

Sample Questionnaire for Evaluating Training

To the participant: Please provide us with your candid opinions about this training program by completing this questionnaire. All responses will remain strictly confidential.

For questions 1 through 10, circle the number in the rating scale that comes closest to your opinion.

1. Length of training program?

    Comment:

    Not at all appropriate 1 2 3 4 5 Extremely appropriate

    _____

    _____

2. Relevance of content?

    Comment:

    Not at all appropriate 1 2 3 4 5 Extremely appropriate

    _____

    _____

3. Discussions/lectures?

    Comment:

    Poor 1 2 3 4 5 Excellent

    _____

    _____

4. Small group sessions?

    Comment:

    Poor 1 2 3 4 5 Excellent

    _____

    _____

5. Audiovisuals (if used)?

    Comment:

    Poor 1 2 3 4 5 Excellent

    _____

    _____

6. Handouts/readings?

    Comment:

    Poor 1 2 3 4 5 Excellent

    _____

    _____

7. Trainer's skills?   Poor   1 2 3 4 5   Excellent

    Comment:

    _____

    _____

8. How much did you benefit from training   Not at all   1 2 3 4 5   Very much
    program?

    Comment:

    _____

    _____

9. What recommendation would you give   Poor   1 2 3 4 5   Excellent
    this training program?

    Comment:

    _____

    _____

10. What did you like best about the training? _____

    _____

    _____

    _____

    _____

11. What did you like least about the training? _____

    _____

    _____

    _____

    _____

12. Additional comments? _____

    _____

    _____

    _____

    _____

Thank you for your participation.

II. Workshops on *The Creative Curriculum for Family Child Care*

This chapter of the *Trainer's Guide* outlines a series of workshops based on *The Creative Curriculum for Family Child Care.* You will find workshops on the content of Setting the Stage and each of the activities in Part Two.

Workshops focused on the *Curriculum* serve two important functions. First, they can be used to introduce providers to the content in a nonthreatening manner. Providers who may be reluctant to pick up the *Curriculum* and use it on their own are thus introduced to its content in small doses as part of a workshop activity. A second advantage to conducting workshops focused on the *Curriculum* is that it enables providers to share their experiences and knowledge with others and to discuss solutions to common problems. Many providers lack opportunities to meet with colleagues to discuss what is happening in their homes. When asked what they value most about a workshop, providers often cite the opportunity to share with others. Thus, the workshops in this chapter include activities that enable providers to work in both large and small groups, to share experiences and knowledge, and to relate what they are learning to their everyday experiences.

To further encourage participation and involvement, providers are sometimes asked to bring something from home to contribute to a workshop. Where appropriate, the workshops include an activity in which providers can make something to take back to their programs. Because most family child care providers work with children who span a range of ages, we have tried to address the challenges that often result from mixed-age grouping. And finally, this chapter offers suggestions for sharing the curriculum with parents.

You can refer back to the previous chapter, Planning Effective Training Sessions, for more detailed planning tips on presentation techniques, agendas, logistical concerns, and so on. It is important to keep this information in mind as you tailor your workshops for your particular group.

Each of the following workshops includes several learning activities. Not all the activities suggested will be appropriate for your group or for you as a trainer. You will need to consider individual learning styles, how much time you have, and the level of experience and expertise of the participants. For example, some groups like to use their imaginations and engage in role playing; others are uncomfortable with these kinds of activities but enjoy group discussions and presentations. If you don't yet know your group well, offering a variety of learning experiences is a good option.

Some workshop activities invite providers to try out children's activities and materials. It is important that you explain why you are doing this, or the providers may think you are wasting their time. Adults sometimes need permission to be childlike and enjoy themselves, and it is important to relate this play to the provider's own work.

Whether they have years of experience or are just starting out, the providers in your group will know a lot simply because they are adults with valuable life experiences. Group discussions and the sharing of ideas allow you to show that you respect this knowledge. At the same time, you as the trainer must be prepared to fill in the gaps and facilitate group discussions. If the group consists of inexperienced providers, they may need more direction and specific information. If you can relate new ideas about high-quality child care to what providers already know, learning will surely take place.

Throughout these workshops, two techniques are often suggested: small group discussions with reports back to the large group, and brainstorming of ideas that are written on a flip chart. As you are planning and implementing your workshops, consider the following suggestions:

- If your group is small (15 people or less), discussions involving the entire group are effective and allow members to hear all the ideas presented.

- Small group discussions are a particularly good way of encouraging shy participants to share their ideas. They offer more intimate connections among class members.

- When asking small groups to report back to the larger group, consider asking each group to present 1 or 2 ideas at first; then go from group to group until all new ideas are listed. This prevents repetitious reporting, and the first group to report doesn't "use up" all the best answers.

- While we often suggest having small groups report on their discussions, you may not always choose to do this. Not reporting supports each small group's sense of uniqueness and reporting may not always be necessary. You may want to suggest that the groups should feel free to share what they have learned informally, at break time.

Finally, welcoming the workshop participants at every session, providing a variety of learning experiences, and offering some closure on each session (perhaps a short review and an idea of what to look forward to) will help ensure a successful series of workshops.

Introductory Workshop

Purpose of the workshop:

To enable participants to get to know other members of the group and to introduce the series of workshops.

In this workshop, participants will:

- play 2 games to introduce themselves to the group;

- discuss the factors that characterize a high-quality program;

- share views on the rewards and challenges of being a family child care provider; and

- learn about the content and format of *The Creative Curriculum for Family Child Care.*

Materials you will need:

- Get Acquainted Lotto cards for each participant (Handout #1);

- name tags;

- a selection of objects (at least one for each participant), such as a ping-pong ball, bandaid, stuffed animal, toothbrush, magic marker, toy bulldozer, scissors, and so on;

- copies of the standards for early childhood programs (Handout #2);

- chart paper, markers, and tape; and

- copies of *The Creative Curriculum for Family Child Care.*

Get Acquainted Lotto

As you greet people entering the room, give them a copy of the Get Acquainted Lotto (Handout #1) and ask them to begin playing the game as you wait for everyone to arrive. Explain that the task is to go around and meet people, ask each person which category (or categories) apply to them, and fill in the lotto card with their names. When everyone has arrived and participated in the game, reconvene the group and find out what people have learned about one another. Summarize what you have learned about the members of the group from this exercise.

Introducing the Workshop

- Explain that participants will begin to know each other and share ideas about family child care and that the workshop series will be introduced.

- Outline the activities for the session.

Me and My Object

This is an enjoyable activity that challenges participants' creativity and enables them to introduce themselves to the group in a nonthreatening way. Pass around your collection of objects and ask each person to select one. Then give the follow instructions:

- Examine your object carefully to learn as much as you can about it: how it feels, smells, works, and so forth. Think about how you would describe your object to someone who couldn't see it.

- Now think about how the object is like you and how it is different from you.

- When you are all ready, each of us will introduce ourselves and our objects to the group by telling how we are like and how we are different from our objects

Here's an example of how someone might introduce herself and her object:

> "I selected a ping-pong ball, which is hard on the outside, smooth, and white. It also bounces a lot if dropped. My name is Mary. I'm like this ping-pong ball in a number of ways. Being a provider, I sometimes feel like this ball. I get knocked around a lot by the children, who make lots of demands on my time. But I can bounce back quickly like this ball. I'm smooth and hard on the outside, but soft inside—sometimes I think I'm too soft and I let parents get away with too much, but that's another story! I've been a family child care provider for 5 years, so like this ping-pong ball, I can last a long time. I have 2 children of my own, ages 8 and 3, and the older one loves to play ping-pong."

Allow time for everyone (including yourself) to make an introduction. Give a brief summary of what you have learned, and emphasize the creativity that people displayed in their introductions.

Activity I: What Is High-Quality Child Care and Why Is Quality Important?

Ask participants to imagine that someone is visiting their family child care home to determine whether it is a high-quality program. What are the key aspects of the program that providers most want visitors to notice? Allow several minutes for each person to think about this question and to write down several ideas. Then invite participants to share what they wrote by calling out items from their lists. As they do so, write the ideas on a chart. Participants may note the following factors:

- a safe and secure environment;

- a place where the children are talked to about what they are doing;

- a home organized to meet the needs of the children;

- good relationships with parents;

- appropriate toys and materials;

- outdoor activities every day;

- good nutritious meals;

- a place where children are helped to feel good about who they are; and

- a place where children are helped to get along with others.

Review the list developed by the group. Then distribute Handout #2, Elements of a High Quality Program. Share with the participants the following list of features of high-quality programs as presented in one of the early publications on this topic. (Phillips, D., (Ed.), *Quality in Child Care: What Does Research Tell Us?* 1987) This book summarized 6 different research studies that examined the characteristics of high-quality programs. The studies identified 4 major features of these programs:

- The physical environment is safe and orderly and contains varied, stimulating toys and educational materials organized into activity areas.

- Children are given freedom to learn—to select activities and to interact with materials, other children, and adults.

- Adults read to children, give choices, and are accepting, informative, and responsive to children's needs.

- Adults have specialized training in child development.

Emphasize that although these studies were done in center-based programs, the same factors apply to family child care homes.

Then share with participants the following publications:

- Bredekamp, S. and Copple, C. (Eds.). (1997). *Developmentally appropriate practice in early childhood programs* (Rev. ed.). Washington, DC: National Association for the Education of Young Children.

- U.S. Department of Health and Human Services. Administration for Children and Families. Administration on Children, Youth and Families. *Head Start Bureau. Head Start program performance standards and other regulations.* (2001). Alexandria, VA: Head Start Information and Publication Center.

- Council for Professional Recognition. *The Child Development Associate assessment system and competency standards for family child care.* (1999). Washington, DC: Author.

Point out that each of these publications lists standards for quality and that the criteria given in each are very similar. It is important to relate the profession's standards to the elements identified by the group so as to validate its ideas. Discuss why a high-quality program is so important: only such programs can really enhance a child's social and cognitive development and have long-term positive effects on a child's development.

Activity II: Meeting the Challenges of Family Child Care

It is useful to begin this activity by acknowledging that although standards help us define quality, they are not always easy to achieve. Ask participants to review the criteria again and think for a few minutes about the greatest barriers to achieving quality in their programs. Suggest that they may want to write down some of their ideas.

Have participants form small groups of 3 or 4 so they can share their barriers. Ask each group to select a "reporter" to record their discussion and report back to the group. Give each reporter a sheet of chart paper and a magic marker. Allow about 10 minutes for participants to discuss barriers to quality. Then reconvene the group and ask the reporters to share their lists. You may hear about barriers such as the following:

- the difficulty of meeting the varied needs of children from birth to age 12;

- problems with including infants and toddlers in activities planned for the older children;

- keeping the house somewhat orderly when caring for toddlers;

- not having funds for sufficient materials and equipment;

- thinking of things to do that are different and fun; and

- getting children outside each day when you don't have a yard.

After all groups have made their reports, summarize what you have heard, and point out how using a curriculum can help providers address many of the barriers they identified. Distribute copies of *The Creative Curriculum for Family Child Care* and refer participants to the introduction, which discusses how a curriculum can support their role. Present a brief overview of the content and format of the Curriculum.

As a conclusion to this introductory session, share your schedule and plan for the series of workshops you will be presenting. Try to relate the content in the *Curriculum* with the issues that participants raised in the discussion. You might also show the videotape *Caring and Learning*, which was filmed in 4 different homes and illustrates how providers offer a range of appropriate activities for young children.

Handout #1

Family Child Care Get Acquainted Lotto		
A provider who serves infants and toddlers.	A provider who has been operating a program for more than 3 years.	A provider who uses a curriculum to plan the program.
A provider with school-age children.	A provider who enjoys cooking with children.	A provider who has helped other providers get started.
A provider who once worked in a center-based program.	A provider who takes the children to story hour at the library.	A provider who has no yard but takes children outside every day.
A new provider who has been in family child care for less than a year.	A provider who has joined a professional organization.	A provider who makes toys and other learning materials for the children.

Handout #2

Elements of a High-Quality Program

Substantial agreement exists in the field of early childhood education on what constitutes high-quality care for young children. Experts agree that a high-quality early childhood program must be developmentally appropriate. This means that:

- children learn at their own pace through active interactions;

- the environment is well planned and includes a rich variety of materials and choices;

- adults ask questions that expand children's play and support a positive self-concept; and

- parents play a meaningful role in the program and have a good understanding of its philosophy and goals.

Standards

Several standards of quality have been established by the early childhood profession. These standards, which specify the criteria for developmental appropriateness, include the following:

- Bredekamp, S. and Copple, C. (Eds.). (1997). *Developmentally appropriate practice in early childhood programs* (Rev. ed.). Washington, DC: National Association for the Education of Young Children.

- Council for Professional Recognition. *The Child Development Associate assessment system and competency standards for family child care.* (1999). Washington, DC: Author.

- Harms, T., & Clifford, R. M. (1989). *Family day care rating scale.* New York: Teachers College Press.

- National Association for Family Child Care. (2003). *The quality standards for National Association for Family Child Care accreditations* (3rd ed.). Salt Lake City, UT: Author.

- U.S. Department of Health and Human Services. Administration for Children and Families. Administration on Children, Youth and Families. Head Start Bureau. *Head Start program performance standards and other regulations.* (2001). Alexandria, VA: Head Start Information and Publication Center.

Child Development as the Foundation for a High-Quality Program

Purpose of the workshop:

To gain an understanding of how children think and learn at each stage of development, and to know what to expect of infants, toddlers, and preschool and school-age children.

In this workshop, participants will:

- look at children's drawings and responses to questions to determine how children think about and make sense of the world;

- discuss typical characteristics of infants, toddlers, preschoolers, and school-age children; and

- consider the importance of understanding child development in planning a developmentally appropriate program.

Materials you will need:

- pictures of What Happens to the Cookie After Someone Eats It (Handout #3);

- index cards with an anecdote on each one (use Handout #4, Anecdotes That Illustrate Children's Thinking);

- the Animism Responses (Handout #5);

- flip chart paper and markers; and

- copies of the *The Creative Curriculum for Family Child Care*.

Introducing the Workshop

- Explain that one of the enjoyable aspects of working with young children is that they have unique ways of explaining and learning about the world around them.

- Indicate that this workshop will involve participants in making their own discoveries about how young children think and learn.

- Outline what you will be doing in this session.

- List on flip chart paper and discuss briefly the following principles regarding how young children think and learn:

    Children have their own view of the world; they see and understand the world differently from adults. To understand children and help them love learning, adults must listen carefully, observe closely, and take children seriously.

    Children learn through their play and by observing carefully what happens around them.

    Children are more likely to remember connections they make themselves.

    Development takes time; trying to hurry children through each stage does not benefit them.

Activity I: How Children View the World

Ask participants to sit at 1 of 3 tables in the room. Each group will have a different set of materials to examine:

- children's drawings of "what happens to the cookie after someone eats it,"

- animism responses, and

- anecdotes written on index cards.

Explain that the purpose of this activity is to look at examples of children's drawings, anecdotes, and responses to a set of questions about what is alive and what is not alive. After reviewing the set of materials on the table, ask each group to respond to the following questions:

- What can you learn about children's thinking?

- How does their thinking change over time?

Allow about 15 minutes for the groups to review each of the 3 sets of materials. Then lead a discussion to summarize their observations.

In discussing participants' observations of how children responded to the task of drawing "what happens to the cookie after someone eats it," you will want to bring out the following points:

- Three- and four-year-old children draw the cookie itself or someone putting the cookie in his or her mouth. They are unable to think of something they have never seen (such as where the cookie goes after it is eaten).

- Five- to seven-year-olds understand that the cookie goes into their bodies, and sometimes they draw the cookie in the stomach.

- Older children (8 to 10) have acquired a broader understanding of body parts and functions and can represent these concepts in great detail.

- Most children draw chocolate chip cookies.

In discussing participants' observations of the Animism Responses, emphasize the following points about young children:

- They believe that if something can move, it is alive.

- They often attribute human attributes to inanimate objects.

- If something is important to them (e.g., a pencil) or powerful (e.g., fire), they think it is alive.

- As children grow older, their information becomes more accurate, but sometimes they have a "cognitive conflict" (e.g., they think something is half alive).

- Children like to share information and knowledge they have acquired if they think an adult is really interested in their ideas.

In discussing participants' conclusions drawn from the anecdote cards, bring out the following points:

- Children seem to make a lot of "errors" in their thinking, but it is really that they think in a different way than adults do.

- By observing children and listening to what they say, we can learn a lot about what young children think and how they view the world around them.

- Giving children the correct response isn't as important as showing that we respect their ideas and understand their way of thinking.

Activity II: Child Development as the Foundation for Curriculum Planning

Explain that *The Creative Curriculum for Family Child Care* is based on child development theory: how children grow socially, emotionally, cognitively, and physically at each stage. In using a child development-based curriculum, providers also must consider what they know of each child's unique abilities, interests, and needs. Tell participants that in this activity you will focus on normal stages of child development and how this information can be used to plan a developmentally appropriate program.

Set up 4 groups, one for each age group—infants, toddlers, preschool children, and school-age children—and have participants select the group they want to focus on. (Encourage participants to try to make the groups fairly equal in size.) Give each group a sheet of chart paper and markers. Explain that they will have 10 minutes to discuss the typical characteristics of children in their age group. Each group should select a reporter who will list the ideas.

Reconvene the large group and invite reporters to present the characteristics of their age groups. After each presentation, refer participants to the section in Part One, Setting the Stage, which shows how curriculum offerings are related to what children are like at each stage of development.

After you have discussed each age group, have participants review the child growth and development charts in Setting the Stage. Ask if there is additional information here that is interesting. Point out that these charts identify norms for development; each child is different and will grow at a slightly different pace. Stress that the charts can be used as a handy reference and as guidelines to consider when planning a program.

Assignment: Encourage participants to review the rest of Part One prior to the next workshop. Suggest that they might want to use the safety checklists to verify the safety of their home. Ask participants to bring a copy of their daily schedule to the next workshop.

Conclusion

Refer the group back to the introductory statements and briefly relate examples of what they said during the session, showing how these support those main ideas.

Handout #3

What Happens to the Cookie After Someone Eats It

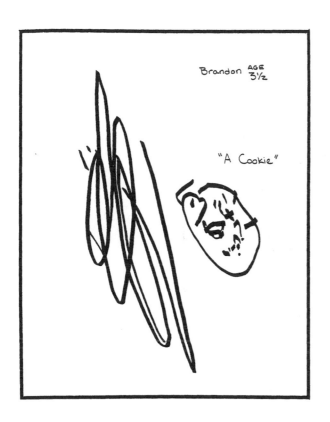

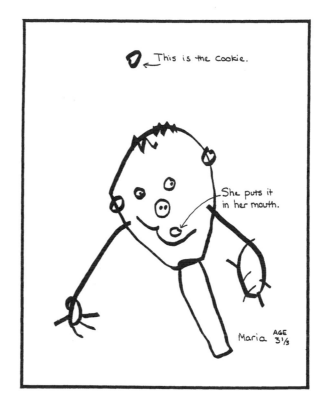

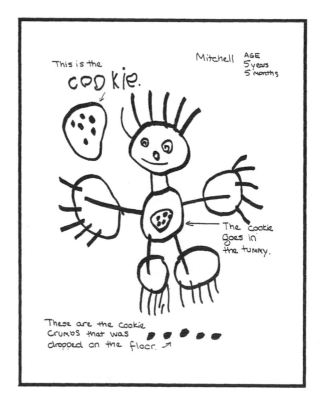

I like to eat cookies. I like to snitch cookies. I take the cookie & I eat it & then it goes into my tummy.

David AGE 7

By amy AGE 8¼

neck tubes
liver
liver
stomach

First you eat the cookie & then it goes down through the neck and goes through all sorts of pipes. After it goes to the stomach the stomach kind of stretches and it settles down in the stomach.

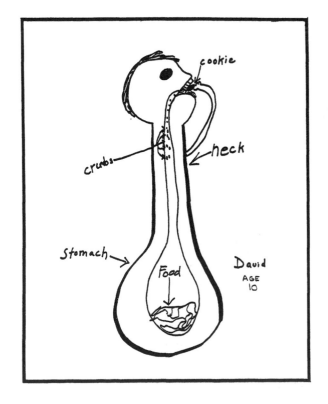

cookie
crubs
neck
Stomach
Food
David AGE 10

Handout #4

Anecdotes That Illustrate Children's Thinking

(Trainers: Copy each of these anecdotes on an index card.)

A provider is playing peek-a-boo using a puppet that pops up behind a blanket. When the provider asks the baby where the puppet is, the child gives clear signs that he doesn't know.

A 4-year-old was walking around with a bag of potato chips that he was squeezing to break up the chips. His mother asked why he was smashing the potato chips. His answer: "to make more."

A child of 4, told she had sharp eyes, felt her eyes with her hands and said to her mother, "But they don't feel sharp."

A 3-year-old noticed some unpopped corn in the bottom of a pan and said, "I guess that popcorn didn't want to pop."

A group of 3-year-olds were discussing the difference between mittens and gloves. Finally one little girl announced with authority, "Mittens are little. When they grow up, they will be gloves."

A young child with a bad tooth was asked if it hurt. He replied, "Yes, can't you feel it?"

Two children were each given an equally large cookie. One child broke his into 4 pieces and announced, "Now I have more than you do."

Handout #5
Animism Responses
(What's Alive and What's Not Alive)

Show the Child the Following Items	Tasanee (Three and a half)	Natasha (Four)
Stone	*Yes, it's alive because it is hot.*	*Alive, because rocks are hard. If you throw rocks people get hurt.*
Pencil	*Yes, it's alive because it can write.*	*Alive, because pencils write.*
Broken Button	*No, because it's broken.*	*Alive, 'cause buttons are on dresses and sometimes on pants.*
Watch	*Yes, it's alive because it can turn.*	*Alive, because when it's time to go it's 8 o'clock.*
Chipped Dish	*No, it's not alive because it's a dish.*	*Alive, because sometimes little girls eat cereal in a bowl.*
Ask the Child About the Following Items		
Bicycle	*Yes! You can ride.*	*Alive, because so many people ride it and bikes are real!*
Chair	*Yes, it's alive because you can sit on it.*	*Alive, because people can sit in chairs and rocking chairs, too.*
Tree	*Yes, it's alive 'cause it can move its leaves, it is moving.*	*Alive, 'cause people shake trees, some trees sleep, and some wake up in the morning.*

Ask the Child About the Following Items	Tasanee (Three and a half)	Natasha (Four)
Sun	*Yes, it's alive 'cause if you touch it it can burn you up and you can get dead.*	*Alive, because it will get hot, and sometimes it will get warm.*
Wind	*Yes, it's alive because it can blow, it moves.*	*Not alive, sometimes it gets cold and makes people cold and freezing.*
Car	*Car, yes it's alive, 'cause it can move.*	*Alive, cause some people can drive cars.*
Fire	*Yes, fire is alive because it can burn you up.*	*Alive, because it burns. Sometimes it burns people up and they put water on it and it makes smoke.*
Dog	*Yes, the dog is alive because it can move and run.*	*Alive, because my dog don't have no training. We have to put him in another school. He jumps and comes in the house and runs upstairs.*
Flower	*No, flowers are not alive. They can't walk.*	*Alive, because people pick flowers, wash them to make them clean and put them in a bowl. Then flowers grow.*
River	*Yes, because sh, sh, sh! it can move.*	*Alive, because people can swim in it.*
Clouds	*Yes, they go slow but look, look! they can move. (She was watching the sky)*	*Alive, because they are brown and white and shiny and bright and they move slow.*
Use this space to record any impressions you have or patterns you notice.		

Handout #5
Animism Responses

Show the Child the Following Items	Lane (Six)	Ricky (Nine)
Stone	*Not alive. Not like the human being.*	*Not alive. Because it's just a rock. It does not have a heart, it doesn't have blood. It doesn't have cells. Rock comes from the earth, they don't feed on anything.*
Pencil	*Not alive.*	*Not alive. It has lead in it. If anything has lead in it it dies.*
Broken Button	*Not alive because it's for sewing.*	*Not alive. It's solid...nothing in it. It does not live. It does not grow.*
Watch	*Kind of...some work by batteries or electricity. Half alive.*	*Not alive. Because it does not have a heart or anything. It's a piece of machinery.*
Chipped Dish	*Not alive.*	*Not alive. If anything alive is chipped a millimeter or centimeter deep, the dirt will cause germs in your body and it it's not taken out, you have to have your arm cut off. When plates are chipped they don't have to have anything cut off.*
Bicycle	*Half alive, because it goes around. But it can't talk like a bird.*	*Not alive. A bicycle does not grow. Everything that is alive, grows. A bicycle has to be used and it must be controlled by man. Living things do not have to be used by man.*

Ask the Child About the Following Items	Lane (Six)	Ricky (Nine)
Chair	*Not alive, except a rocking chair. It's half...or one that goes around, but it doesn't talk.*	*Not alive. Because a chair is motionless and does not grow.*
Tree	*Yes, it's alive. Well, half because it's not a human being.*	*Alive. Because it grows and has a bark like human skin.*
Sun	*Half alive. Doesn't really move.*	*Not alive. Because it is a star and if anything is that hot it will burn like the sun.*
Wind	*Half alive. Not like us.*	*Not alive. A wind is caused when warm air goes under cold air at the equator.*
Car		*Not alive. It's a piece of machinery and does not grow.*
Fire	*Half alive, the flames can kill someone.*	*Not alive. Because it is when wood burns and wood is usually dead when you put it in the fire.*
Dog	*Alive because it barks, eats, sleeps and lives.*	*Alive. Because it grows.*
Flower	*Half alive. I don't know why.*	*Alive. Because it starts with a little seedling and grows into a nice pretty flower.*
River	*Half alive, fish and waterfalls and boats make it move.*	*Not alive. Because water comes from a spring and it flows into a river. But it does grow.*

Ask the Child About the Following Items	Lane (Six)	Ricky (Nine)
Clouds	*Half alive.*	*Not alive. Because clouds are only mist made of water that steams up from the ground.*
Use this space to record any impressions you have or patterns you notice.		

Setting the Stage

Purpose of the workshop:

To assist providers in establishing an appropriate and interesting home environment and in managing their daily program.

In this workshop, participants will:

- consider how different environments affect behavior;

- discuss appropriate toys and materials for each age group;

- share ideas for selecting, displaying, and storing materials; and

- discuss scheduling and daily routines in family child care.

Materials you will need:

- chart paper, markers, and tape and

- slides you have taken in a family child care home to illustrate ways of organizing space and materials, and/or the videotape *Caring and Learning*.

What providers should bring:

- an object that children especially love to play with and

- their daily schedule, written on chart paper.

Introducing the Workshop

- Explain that *The Creative Curriculum for Family Child Care* emphasizes activities that can be easily implemented in a home setting.

- State that the first step in implementing the *Curriculum* is to create an appropriate environment for the program.

- Review the purpose of the workshop and what you plan to do.

Activity I: Environments Can Frustrate or Support You

Open the activity by stating that we are all affected by our physical environment, sometimes negatively and sometimes positively. In a family child care program, the environment can support what we want to see happening, or it can work against our goals.

Ask participants to close their eyes and think of a store they really hate to shop in. Visualize what the store looks like; what they hear; how it smells; and how they feel as they try to shop in the store. Allow a few minutes, then ask people to share what they were thinking.   You may hear ideas such as the following:

Unattractive displays
Cluttered and disorganized
Difficult to find what I want
Long waits
Can't reach the items
Unpleasant odors
Narrow aisles
Dark and dingy
No logical order to displays
Poor selection
Noisy
Unhelpful salespeople
Loud music

Now ask participants to think of another store where they really like to shop—a pleasant and easy place to shop. Ask them to share some of the characteristics of this second store. Participants will often share ideas such as the following:

Attractive and inviting displays
Everything within reach
Clean and well kept
Soft music
Well organized
Helpful salespeople
Soft carpeting
Well lit
Well-run checkouts

Discuss how the different store environments make us feel and how much easier it is to shop in an attractive and well-organized environment. Then discuss whether any of these same characteristics, positive and negative, can apply to the organization of the home environment for a family child care program.

Activity II: Making Life Hard for Everyone

Explain that you are going to be doing a "reverse brainstorming" activity. Post a list of behaviors that children demonstrate when they are frustrated, and invite participants to add to the list. You might include the following:

Fighting over toys
Throwing toys and materials
Destroying items belonging to the family
Wandering aimlessly
Seeming bored
Showing fear of naptime
Running around in the house
Crying, hitting, or yelling

Then challenge the group to think of the types of environments that would encourage these kinds of behaviors. List all the ideas that come from the brainstorming session. These may include some of the following:

Providing only a few toys
Allowing infants and toddlers to interfere with activities for older children
Moving the furniture so children can run around in circles
Keeping all toys from the children's reach so they have to ask for what they need
Making children sleep in a dark and isolated room
Keeping toys and materials in toy chests
Allowing children to go wherever they want in the house
Keeping out the same toys all the time

Have participants take out their copies of the *Creative Curriculum* and review the sections on setting up an appropriate environment and identifying problems in Setting the Stage. Discuss some of the ideas presented in the *Curriculum* for creating an appropriate environment.

Activity III: Selecting, Displaying, and Storing Toys and Materials

Remind participants that one of the characteristics of high-quality programs is a rich variety of materials and toys that are appropriate for the children who are served and and that are also well-organized and displayed. Acknowledge that it can be expensive to purchase a lot of equipment, but stress that there are other ways to obtain materials.

Invite participants to share with the group an item in their family child care home that the children especially love. Discuss why it is popular with children and how it is used. Review the discussion in Part One of the *Creative Curriculum* on selecting toys and materials. Invite participants to share ways that they have obtained appropriate materials inexpensively. Allow time for participants to review the list of suggested materials to purchase, collect, or make for each age group. You might suggest that they check the items they have and star the ones they would like to obtain.

Emphasize how the display and storage of materials and toys can help children learn to respect and use them purposefully. If you have taken slides of family child care home environments, share these with the group to illustrate arrangements that work as well as those that do not. Alternatively, you might show the videotape *Caring and Learning* and have participants identify how the 4 providers have organized materials and offered choices to children.

Activity IV: Managing the Day

A family child care provider has to be a good manager. A schedule can help organize the day, but it should allow for flexibility. Invite participants to share how they manage their daily program.

Provide masking tape and invite participants who brought copies of their daily schedule to tape them up on the wall. Discuss similarities and differences, what works and what are the problem periods of the day. Refer participants to the sample schedule in Part One of the *Curriculum* and the discussion of challenging times such as meal times, rest time, early morning, mid-afternoon, and the end of the day. If time allows and interest is high, suggest that participants who want to revise and improve their schedules can work together with your assistance.

Conclusion

Explain that in future workshops, you will be focusing on each of the activities described in Part Two of *The Creative Curriculum for Early Childhood*. If you can be flexible about the order of the workshops you will be offering, invite participants to identify their priorities; there is no set order that must be followed.

Dramatic Play

Purpose of the workshop:

To develop an appreciation for the importance of dramatic play and to learn ways of encouraging imaginative play in family child care.

In this workshop, participants will:

- discuss how dramatic play supports development;

- explore a variety of props and materials that can enhance dramatic play;

- discuss the use of prop boxes; and

- review ways of sharing dramatic play with parents.

Materials you will need:

- an assortment of interesting props to stimulate dramatic play, such as an alarm clock, cordless shaver, old typewriter, steering wheel, fabric in bright colors, grocery bags, sleeping bag, stamp pad, fishing pole, and so on;

- paper and markers; and

- situation cards.

What providers should bring:

- an object that they think is particularly good for stimulating children's imaginative play; and

- any prop boxes they have made that the children particularly like.

Introducing the Workshop

- Emphasize that dramatic play is one of the most important activities as well as the easiest to provide.

- Explain the purpose of the workshop and what you plan to do.

Activity I: What Children Learn from Dramatic Play

Ask each participant to think of a situation during the last week in which they observed a child engaged in dramatic play. You might need to offer some examples, such as a toddler taking care of a doll, wearing a fire hat, or using a tablecloth for a cape, or a baby making faces into a mirror.

Ask questions such as the following:

- What was the child saying or doing?

- Was the child playing alone or interacting with others?

- How long did the play go on?

Next, divide the group into 4 teams and give each team a piece of chart paper. Assign each team an area of development (social, emotional, cognitive, and physical) and have them list ways that dramatic play experiences promote children's growth in that area of development. The section in the *Curriculum* on helping children learn through dramatic play may be helpful. Have each group present its ideas and be prepared to expand on them if necessary. Here are some suggestions:

Social Development

- Children learn to play together.

- They try out different roles: for example, doctor, firefighter, mommy and daddy.

- They have to cooperate in order to play.

Emotional Development

- They work out their feelings (e.g., by hitting the doll baby).

- They re-enact scary experiences to help them cope.

- They feel good about themselves.

Cognitive Development

- They try out their ideas.

- They learn new information from other children.

- They solve problems.

- They acquire language skills and expand their vocabularies.

Physical Development

- They develop small muscle skills putting on dress-up clothes.

- They play actively and use their large muscles.

Activity II: Sharing Props

Invite participants to share the prop they brought to the workshop and describe what age group it most appeals to and how it was used. Encourage participants to talk about what they do to stimulate dramatic play.

Then share the props that you have brought to the workshop and discuss some of the suggestions in the *Curriculum* for displaying dramatic play materials.

Activity III: Getting Involved in Dramatic Play

Explain that this activity will focus on how important it is for participants to get involved in children's dramatic play. Divide everyone into teams and give each team a situation card. Ask them to read the card and discuss the question posed.

Situation #1

Two preschoolers are playing in the housekeeping corner. They are serving each other breakfast. A toddler comes in and accidentally knocks the plates off the table. The preschoolers are upset. What can you say and do to rectify the situation and include the toddler in the dramatic play?

Situation #2

An infant enrolled in your program enjoys looking at herself in the mirror. What can you say and do to extend this dramatic play? How could you involve the infant in dramatic play with the other children?

Situation #3

A toddler is carrying a stuffed dog around in his arms. You ask him what the dog's name is and he says, "Rover, and he sick." What can you do and say to extend this child's dramatic play?

Allow 5 to 10 minutes for each group to discuss its ideas on how to handle the situation. Then invite a representative from each group to briefly describe the situation and the group's ideas.

As a conclusion to this activity, ask participants to read the section on involving children of different ages at the end of the chapter on Dramatic Play in the *Creative Curriculum*. Have them share ideas for engaging children of different ages in dramatic play.

Activity IV: Creating Prop Boxes

Explain that one way to encourage dramatic play is by using prop boxes to introduce new themes. Discuss with participants when it might be appropriate to introduce new themes. Some suggestions might include the following:

- when children seem bored with the usual props for dramatic play;

- when children have had a new experience, such as the birth of a baby, moving, a field trip, or an illness in the family; and

- when an exciting event interests the children, such as a special holiday or a fire in the neighborhood.

Introduce the idea of prop boxes and explain that they contain materials that will stimulate children's dramatic play on a particular theme. Share a prop box you have put together, and invite participants to share any prop boxes they have brought.

Have participants review the section on making prop boxes in the chapter on Dramatic Play. Ask for other ideas of prop boxes that would interest the children in their program, and discuss what materials might go into these prop boxes. Finally, discuss possible sources for these materials, such as the following:

- parents (this is an excellent way to involve them);
- grandparents (they often have wonderful things around the house);
- used-clothing stores;
- yard sales;
- stores that may be willing to donate things; and
- organizations such as a fire house, beauty shop, or pet store.

Ask each person to pick one prop box that he or she would like to develop and write down items that could be collected for the box. Suggest setting up a system for exchanging prop boxes.

Activity V: Sharing Dramatic Play with Parents

Parents are an excellent resource for props and dress-up clothes that inspire dramatic play. They are also interested in learning about their child's imaginative play. Review with participants the letter to parents at the end of the chapter on Dramatic Play, and discuss other ways in which they might share the same information with parents. Invite participants to share some of the ways they have involved parents in dramatic play activities.

Conclusion

Close the workshop with encouraging words such as these: "In this workshop we've shared many ideas for extending children's play, and we've reminded ourselves how important dramatic play is for children's development. I hope each of you has fun trying out a new idea in the next week with the children in your care."

Blocks

Purpose of the workshop:

To emphasize the importance of block play for children of all ages, and to provide an opportunity for participants to make a set of milk carton blocks for the program.

In this workshop, participants will:

*   play with blocks and discuss what children learn from their block play;

*   identify how children learn math concepts and solve problems with blocks;

*   build a set of milk carton blocks; and

*   discuss ideas for involving parents.

Materials you will need:

*   a variety of types of blocks suitable for children of different ages:

>   cloth-covered spongy blocks
>   cardboard
>   wooden unit blocks (some activities require many unit blocks)
>   milk carton blocks

*   labeled storage shelves and a toy box or cardboard box;

*   materials for making cardboard blocks:

>   cardboard milk cartons (2 for each size block)
>   newspapers
>   rubber bands
>   contact paper to cover the finished product (solid colors only)
>   scissors for each person or paper cutters; and

*   instruction cards for the block play activity.

What providers should bring:

*   samples of the blocks they use in their program and

*   cardboard milk cartons of various sizes.

Introducing the Workshop

- Explain that participants will have an opportunity to play with different types of blocks and to discuss what children learn in block play.

- Review the purpose of the workshop and what you plan to do.

Activity I: Experiencing Block Play

If you are working with providers who have little or no experience in offering block play, this workshop can be quite helpful. If you think your group is a bit more advanced, a short presentation on what children learn from block play would probably be a better workshop choice. Be sure to include all age groups in your presentations.

Set up different stations for each type of block you have collected. Allow ample space for the unit blocks and hollow blocks if you have them. Invite participants to select the blocks that interest them the most and begin playing with them. Note that there is no right way to use the blocks; people should explore and build in any ways they want. Tell them that you will be playing the role of the provider, and as participants use the different blocks, walk around to observe, comment on what they are doing, and ask questions to extend their ideas. If time permits, have participants move to another area to experience a different type of block. When it seems appropriate, lead a discussion on block play. Offer some of your observations, including quotes from the participants as they were building. Ask if these comments give clues as to what learning is taking place. Use questions such as these:

- What could children learn playing with blocks as you did?

- Which types of blocks offer the most opportunities for learning for infants, toddlers, preschool children, and school-age children?

Refer participants to the first section of the chapter on Blocks to review the importance of blocks and how block play contributes to all areas of a child's development.

Activity II: Learning Math Concepts Through Block Play

If you have a set of unit blocks and want to encourage providers to use them in their program, this activity is very appropriate. It should be made clear to the providers that the activity focuses on preschool and older children. Begin by demonstrating for participants that unit blocks are so named because they are scaled to a unit size; 2 squares equal 1 unit, 2 units equal 1 double unit, and so on. Point out that there are other, less obvious mathematical relationships that children discover through play with unit blocks. To illustrate, ask participants to divide into 2 teams and work on one of the following tasks:

- How many ways can you find to show math concepts or relationships with blocks (for example, 4 units equal 1 quadruple unit)?

- How many ways can you find to make a variety of geometric shapes with unit blocks?

Allow approximately 5 to 10 minutes (depending on how involved the groups become). When participants are through, allow each team to share its discoveries with the rest of the group. Note all responses on the flip chart and add any that you observed.

In summarizing the experience, be sure to make the following points:

- Children discover many concepts through block play, including spatial relations, measurement and size, volume, and weight.

- Teachers can extend children's experiences by helping them identify and name the many concepts they discover. For example:

  What blocks are used: "You found out that 2 of these blocks make 1 long block."
  Where the blocks were placed: "You used 4 blocks to make a big square."
  How many blocks were used: "You used all the blocks to make the road."

Activity III: Solving Problems Through Block Play

Explain that children create and then solve many problems for themselves through block play. They learn to negotiate, compromise, and cooperate. They also solve problems that relate to math, physics, and structure. To give participants firsthand experience in what young children do, assign each team one of the following tasks:

1. Build a ramp leading to a bridge.
2. Find a way to make 5 steps leading to a building.
3. Create a house with windows and a roof.
4. Build an apartment house with an elevator.
5. Make a "map" of your neighborhood using blocks.

Allow at least 15 minutes but preferably more time to provide for full involvement. Be sure to have lots of blocks available for use. As participants work, write down anything they say that illustrates a specific concept or skill that children develop through block play. Because this exercise is a cooperative one, pay close attention to examples of social skills and language development that you observe.

As you rotate among the groups, ask questions or comment on what you see, just as you want providers to do as they work with children in their homes.

When the tasks are completed, lead a discussion of the problems that participants encountered and how they solved them. You might begin with questions such as these:

- How did you solve the problem you were assigned?

- Was it more complicated than you thought?

- How do you think a child would have approached the same problem?

- What kinds of problems would younger children be addressing during block building?

As a follow-up, suggest that providers who have unit blocks in their homes observe what children do and note examples of the problem-solving they see.

To clean up the blocks, have half the group put their blocks on a labeled shelf and the other half in a toy box or cardboard carton. Then ask each group to identify the advantages and disadvantages of each type of storage.

The group using the box for storage might note the following:

- It was faster putting away the blocks in a box.

- It was very noisy.

- When blocks are in a box, you can't find what you need.

The group placing blocks on the labeled shelves might make the following observations:

- It was satisfying to know I was putting them in the correct place.

- It took longer.

- Putting the blocks on the shelf was fun—matching shapes made it into a game.

- I was matching shapes with a label.

Activity IV: Blocks to Take Home

This is an optional activity for participants who are interested in a make-and-take workshop and who want to try out milk carton blocks in their program. The directions are in the *Creative Curriculum* in the chapter on Blocks. You might first demonstrate the process and then assist participants in making their own blocks. Be sure to have a sufficient quantity of milk cartons (half-pint, pint, quart, and half-gallon) and newspapers on hand. It will be a lot easier to cut the newspaper to size if you have a paper cutter available.   This activity will take approximately 45 minutes to an hour.

Activity V: How Do We Involve Parents?

Discuss the letter to parents and how it might be used. If some providers do not feel that the letter would be appropriate for their parents, discuss other ways to help parents understand the value of block play. Questions such as the following might stimulate a discussion:

- How do you think parents view blocks?

- What could you do to help parents appreciate the value of block experiences?

- How can parents help you obtain blocks for your program?

Conclusion

Refer participants to the *Creative Curriculum* for ideas on building blocks or acquiring them inexpensively. Let participants know what to look forward to in upcoming workshops.

Toys

Purpose of the workshop:

To demonstrate how to select and use toys that support development in infants, toddlers, preschoolers, and school-age children.

In this workshop, participants will:

- evaluate the characteristics of good and bad toys;

- identify ways to support children's growth and development through the use of various toys;

- examine and use homemade toys and collectibles; and

- discuss ways to convey the value of appropriate toys to parents.

Materials you will need:

- a selection of good toys for infants, toddlers, preschoolers, and school-age children (see the chapter on Toys) and

- samples of homemade toys and collections such as plastic bottle caps, keys, shells, buttons, and plastic bag tabs.

What providers should bring:

- a toy they especially like using with children and

- a homemade toy.

Introducing the Workshop

- Note that everyone who cares for young children has toys, but providers don't always get to choose the ones they most want.

- Explain that this workshop will focus on appropriate toys and how they can promote children's growth and development.

- Review your plans for the workshop.

Activity I: Characteristics of Good Toys

Ask participants if they can remember some of the toys that were their favorites when they were children. Be prepared to share your own favorite toys first, if necessary. Summarize the ideas that emerge from this discussion.

Next, invite participants to share the toy they like using with children and explain why they think children especially like the toy. You may want to begin listing the characteristics of toys that emerge from this discussion, including the following possibilities:

Can be used in many different ways
Holds the child's interest
Stimulates imaginative play
Encourages children to think
Creates opportunities to solve problems
Can be used by children of all ages

Invite participants to examine the toys you have displayed for the workshop. Ask them to identify which of the criteria that you listed are met by each of the toys. Emphasize that toys are tools for learning; often the same toy can be used in different ways, depending on the age of the child. For example, infants will put nesting blocks in their mouths and bang them on the floor, while toddlers will fill them with objects and dump them out again. Preschoolers are more likely to fit them together or build with them.

Refer participants to the chapter on Toys, which lists appropriate toys for each age group. You might discuss the idea of setting up a toy lending library if this is feasible.

Activity II: My Worst Toy

Ask each participant to think of the worst toy they have purchased or received as a gift, either for their own children or for their program. Invite each person to name the toy and tell why it was a bad purchase. Make a list of the characteristics of these toys. They may include the following:

Easily broken
Unsafe
Only one use
Did not hold children's interest
Did not promote creativity
Was not appealing
Promoted values I did not approve of

Summarize the discussion by stating that these experiences help us know what toys to acquire by showing us what to avoid.

Activity III: What Children Can Learn from Good Toys

Using the toys that you collected for the workshop, have participants select one they like and work with a partner to identify what children can learn from the toy. Invite them first to simply explore and play with the toy. Then list the following questions to be addressed by each pair:

- How would this toy be used by an infant, a toddler, a preschooler, and a school-age child?

- What could children of different ages learn (socially, emotionally, physically and cognitively) by using this toy?

- How could you use the toy with children to help them learn new skills and concepts?

Allow time for each group to report on their toys and add to their ideas if necessary.

Activity IV: Using Collections and Homemade Toys

On a flip chart, list some of the advantages of using homemade materials:

- They can be tailored to meet the needs of children in your group.

- They can be designed to teach and reinforce a specific skill or concept.

- They are an inexpensive way to enrich your program.

Invite participants who brought a homemade toy to share it with the group and to describe how it is used by children and what they believe children learn by using the toy.

Display the homemade materials you have collected, including objects such as bottle caps, keys, seeds, buttons, plastic tabs, and shells. Select a collection that you have in ample supply (for example, bottle caps), and ask each participant to select one they especially like. Then say:

- Look at the bottle cap carefully and identify all its characteristics.

- Now find someone who has a cap that's like yours in one way.

- Can you form a group of 3 caps?

- Now see how many ways you can develop new groups of caps.

Summarize the exercise by reviewing what participants need to do and know to complete the task (i.e., identify likenesses and differences and classify or group objects accordingly). Learning to classify like objects is an important thinking skill that children develop and refine when they play with toys.

Have participants form groups of 4 each. Give each group a set of "collectibles" (e.g., keys, buttons, plastic fasteners, seashells). The participants' task is to figure out as many ways as possible to group the objects. Allow approximately 10 minutes for the activity and then ask each group to share its categories. Summarize the foregoing activities by suggesting that participants make these or other "collectibles" available in their homes and see what children do with them.

Activity V: Sharing Toys with Parents

Most parents are interested in what their children are learning when they play with toys. Parents are also a potential resource for used toys, which they may be willing to share or loan to the program.

Ask participants to share their ideas on how and when they communicate with parents about toys. Here are some ideas you might add to the discussion:

- Distribute copies of brochures on selecting toys and on safety issues.

- Put up a sign asking for toy donations.

- Ask for donations of objects for collections (e.g., shells, ribbons, buttons).

- Establish a parent bulletin board and post articles on toy safety, homemade toys, or criteria for selecting toys.

- Around the holidays, give parents suggestions for appropriate toys.

Conclusion

Summarize the workshop's content in a few sentences, perhaps referring to the providers' lists of characteristics of good toys and how toys can be used for learning experiences.

Art

Purpose of the workshop:

To encourage providers to use all kinds of art media to promote children's creativity and self-esteem.

In this workshop, participants will:

- examine the developmental stages of children's art;

- experience a developmentally inappropriate art activity;

- try out different art activities and discuss them;

- discuss ways of talking with children about their attitude; and

- discuss barriers to providing successful art activities and ways of sharing art with parents.

Materials you will need:

- a detailed coloring book commonly found in any grocery store;

- crayons; and

- materials needed to set up work areas for making play dough, painting, printing, and collage.

What providers should bring:

- sample drawings made by the children in their program (all ages) and

- recipes for art materials that work well (e.g., finger paint, play dough, glue, silly putty).

Introducing the Workshop

- State that art activities are enjoyed by almost all children and that they also promote children's growth in all areas of development.

- Emphasize that the process of art is more important to children than making a product and that it is very important for adults to remember this in planning art experiences for children.

- Review what you plan to do in the workshop.

Activity I: Developmental Stages of Children's Art

Prior to the workshop, tape signs on the walls indicating each age group: infants, toddlers, preschoolers, and school-age children. Have masking tape or push pins available.

Invite participants to share the drawings and paintings they have collected for the workshop. Tape or pin each drawing under the sign indicating the age of the child. Discuss the differences in children's abilities at each stage, and ask participants for their ideas on why it is important to allow children to be creative in their artwork. List the ideas that are shared, which may include the following:

- Children experience a sense of accomplishment by doing their own work.

- They put their ideas into concrete form.

- They express their own ideas.

- Art activities allow children to develop and refine their small muscle skills and eye/hand coordination.

- All their senses are involved.

- They learn to make choices, work independently, try out ideas, and experiment.

Activity II: A Developmentally Inappropriate Art Activity

(A note of caution: Some participants may be annoyed by this activity. Be aware that many like coloring books; therefore, avoid being too negative about their use.)

To demonstrate how young children feel when art activities are inappropriate, distribute the coloring book and ask participants to rip out a picture they like. Provide a selection of crayons and give the following directions:

- Select a color you like.

- If you are right-handed, put the crayon in your left hand; if you are left-handed, put the crayon in your right hand.

- Now color the design as carefully as you can, being sure to stay in the lines.

As participants are working on the coloring assignment, walk around the room and make comments such as the following:

- Try a little harder to stay in the lines.

- Look how nicely _____ is coloring her design.

- Hurry up; we're almost out of time.

- Have you ever seen anyone with green hair?

After several minutes of this activity, participants will probably express their frustrations freely. Now offer blank sheets of paper and tell participants they can color whatever they would like, using as many different colors as they wish.

After they are finished, lead a discussion by asking:

- What did you experience in the second activity (for instance, freedom, large movement, fun)?

- What did you experience in the first activity (for instance, pressure, boredom, working hard to please the teacher)?

Ask participants to identify all the advantages of child-initiated art and all the advantages of coloring books. Record the ideas on chart paper. Your chart may look something like the one below.

Child-initiated art	Coloring books
Expression of own ideas Development of creativity Experience of a sense of pride ("I can do it myself") Free use of color Representation of ideas on paper (reading and math readiness)	Development of small muscle control Practice in following directions Learning to stay in the lines

Point out how the things that children can learn from creative art experiences differ from what they learn from coloring books. Note that although coloring books may offer the opportunity to learn certain skills, it is unlikely that the child will develop creative expression through their use.

Activity III: Exploring Art Materials

Tell the providers that you are going to try a role play in which they can have fun and not say one word.

Set up a variety of art materials and activities at several tables. These might include painting, making and using play dough, collage and glue, printing, and weaving. Invite participants to experiment with some of the materials you have set out. They can stay with a single media or try them all if they wish. Explain that while they are working, you will demonstrate ways of talking with children to extend their learning as they engage in art activities. Then rotate from one area to another and comment on what participants are doing. Use this opportunity to model how you want participants to respond to children's efforts. Here are some examples of what you might say:

- You have been working very hard.

- Would you like to tell me about your picture?

- You used all kinds of things on your collage.

- How could you make the play dough less sticky?

- Can you tell me how you made that color?

Give participants a 10-minute warning before it's time to clean up.

- Ten more minutes until we need to clean up.

- You have time to try one more activity.

- Think about what else you want to add to your collage, because in a few minutes it will be time to clean up.

After cleaning up, convene the group to discuss their experiences: what they liked about the activity and what they learned. Share your own observations and the comments you overheard as participants worked in each area exploring the art materials. Relate your observations to what they should be looking for when they observe children. For example, they should note:

- what materials children of different ages use;

- how children use the materials;

- whether children work alone or with others;

- how long children remain at a task; and

- whether they are ready for more challenging art experiences.

Activity IV: Talking with Children About Their Artwork

Begin the discussion by asking participants what they noticed about the comments you made to them as they explored the art materials. Point out that your comments focused on the process and that you avoided making judgments. You described what you observed—for example:

- what colors they used;

- their actions in exploring the materials;

- the problems they encountered and solved; and

- their discoveries.

You also asked open-ended questions to encourage thinking, such as the following:

- How did you get that straw to stay up?

- What would happen if you mixed these two colors?

- How could make the play dough less sticky?

- Tell me how you made that.

You avoided saying:

- What color is this?

- That's pretty?

- What did you make?

- Try not to use so much glue.

Point out that what we say to children who are engaged in art activities will vary depending on their age and what we know about each child. To practice ways of talking with children, divide the group into 4 teams. Each team will take one of the 4 age groups: infants, toddlers, preschoolers, and school-age children. Considering the activities that the participants just tried, select 2 that would be appropriate for each team's age group. Have each team list 3 comments that they could make or questions they would ask children in their group who are engaged in these activities. Allow 10 minutes for this activity, then invite each team to share its ideas.

Activity V: Barriers to Successful Art Experiences

As a group, brainstorm all the things that get in the way of including art activities in a family child care program. List the ideas on a chart. Then review each problem and have participants identify solutions.

Activity VI: Sharing Art with Parents

One problem that providers often face is helping parents appreciate the value of creative art as opposed to prepared or product-oriented art. Form small working groups and give each group the following situation to discuss.

*Suppose you firmly believe that art should reflect the children's thoughts and feelings—not those of adults. Billy Z's parents let you know they are distressed because they never have any nice coloring-book drawings or models to display around their homes, as do their friends who have children at the "Center." You try talking to the Zs about your philosophy, but it seems to fall on deaf ears. When Mrs. Z makes another critical remark, you share with her an article in **Young Children** that nicely spells out the point of view that dittos and teacher-made models are harmful for children's creativity. Mrs. Z doesn't mention the article to you, so after several days you ask her if she or Mr. Z have any reaction to the article. She murmurs, "It was probably written by some teacher who couldn't draw and was afraid the kids would do better than she could." What should you do now?*

Allow about 10 minutes for the group to discuss the situation and come up with strategies for handling the problem.

Conclusion

Restate the purpose of this workshop to the participants and, if possible, let providers take home unused art materials.

Books

Purpose of the workshop:

To inspire an interest in high-quality children's books and identify effective ways to use books in a family child care setting.

In this workshop, participants will:

- discuss the value of sharing books with children;

- develop criteria for selecting good books for children;

- learn new ways to use books in their family child care home;

- discuss story-reading techniques;

- share flannel board stories and homemade books;

- explore ways of enhancing storytelling; and

- discuss ways of sharing books with parents.

Materials you will need:

- large paper, tape, and markers;

- a selection of good books for infants, toddlers, preschoolers, and school-age children;

- your favorite children's book; and

- situation cards, pencils, and paper.

What providers should bring:

- a favorite book for each age group (infants, toddlers, preschoolers, and school-age children) and

- homemade books or a flannel board story they have made.

Introducing the Workshop

- Discuss the value of books and the role they can play in child development.

- Emphasize that the best way to prepare children to be successful readers is to tell stories and read books to them every day.

- Review what you plan to do in the workshop.

Activity I: The Value of Sharing Books with Children

Share 1 or 2 positive experiences that you had as a child with books. Describe the setting, your feelings, and a little bit about a special book. (If you don't have personal stories to tell, ask colleagues for stories you can share.) Then ask if anyone would like to share what they remember about books and reading as a small child. You may hear responses such as the following:

- I loved books with repetition and rhyme.

- I felt close to my grandmother when she read to me.

- It was a special time when my father told me stories.

- I can still see the beautiful pictures in my mind.

- I was able to escape through books.

You may have some participants who are unable to remember any positive experiences with books. Ask them if they are willing to share their experiences with the group. Ask these participants what could have been done differently to encourage them to enjoy books and reading. This discussion may give everyone insight into what not to do with books!

Point out that studies show that one of the most effective ways to encourage an interest in learning to read is to read to young children every day. Emphasize that this is important for children of all ages. Looking at books and listening to stories opens up many new opportunities and experiences for young children. Ask each person to name one thing that children learn through books. Write these ideas on the the board or on a large piece of flip chart paper. Refer participants to the section on how books support development in the chapter on Books, and discuss the examples of how children benefit from books.

Activity II: How to Choose Good Books for Children

Begin this workshop with a short discussion on where books can be obtained. Answers may include:

Grocery stores	Contributions from parents
Discount stores	Homemade
Bookstores	Used book stores
Toy stores	Hand-me-downs from relatives and friends
Yard sales	Fast-food restaurants
Library	Drugstores

Point out that there are thousands of books available for children, and they can be obtained almost anywhere. However, the content, format, illustrations, and values promoted may not be appropriate for the children in a particular program.

Ask participants to put the books they brought with them in 4 piles: one each for infants, toddlers, preschoolers, and school-age children. Add the books you brought to the relevant piles.

Have participants select the age groups they want to consider and to form 4 associated groups. Have each group read through the books and discuss the following questions:

- Is the book appropriate for the age group and why?

- What would children like about the book?

- How would you use the book with children?

- How might another age group use or enjoy this book?

Give each group a large piece of paper and have each develop criteria for selecting books for children in its age group. These criteria can come from providers' discussions of the books they know as well as from their own experiences in using books with children.

Have each group tape its list on the wall, and invite each to share its criteria. Refer to the section on selecting books in the chapter on Books. Suggest that participants may want to write down their ideas and share them with parents or put them on a bulletin board.

Refer participants to the appendix of the chapter on Books. Review the list with participants, sharing what you know about the books and identifying your own favorites. Invite participants to do the same. Encourage participants to write down the titles of 2 books they would most like to have for each age group and where they will obtain them.

Note to the Trainer: This might be an appropriate time to discuss setting up a book lending library.

Activity III: Using Books in Family Child Care

Divide participants into groups of 3 to 5 people, and give each group one of the situation cards. Ask each group to choose a reporter who will take notes on its discussion and report back to the large group.

Situation #1

In your family child care program you presently have an infant, 2 toddlers, 2 preschoolers, and a school-age child. You have a scheduled story time when the children arrive in the morning before they have a snack. You are finding it difficult to get through the entire story because the infant is fussy and the toddlers get bored easily and leave. This is frustrating for the preschoolers because they want to hear the end of the story, and frustrating for you because you know how important it is to read to young children and expose them to books.

Discuss this situation with the members of the group and come up with ideas on how you can solve this problem.

Situation #2

Discuss all the places that books are kept and used in your family child care program. Describe the ways in which you use books in your program, why it works, and how it involves (if it does) children of different ages. Refer to the section on supporting children's growth and development in the Books chapter of the *Curriculum* if you need additional ideas. Make a chart to summarize all the ideas that are shared.

Situation #3

You have been a family child care provider for 1 year, and your book collection is an odd assortment of books belonging to your own children and ones you have picked up at grocery and discount stores. You are tired of them, and so are the children. You do not have a lot of money to spend on books because you have just bought some new table toys. As a group, brainstorm various ways you can increase and/or change the books you have available. Helpful information can also be found in the section on selecting books in the *Curriculum*.

Give each small group time to share its situation and solutions with the large group.

Activity IV: Story-Reading Techniques

Select a book you particularly like that will enable you to demonstrate the story-reading techniques listed in the section on some guidance on reading with children in the *Curriculum*. A book for older toddlers or preschoolers is best for this activity. After you are finished, ask participants if they liked the story. Why would children like it? Ask them what techniques they noticed you use as you read the story. Refer them to the appropriate section of the *Curriculum*.

Activity V: Flannel Board Stories and Homemade Books

Invite participants who brought their own flannel board stories to present them to the group and demonstrate how they use flannel boards with children. Add that children especially like using the flannel pieces, and suggest that after presenting a flannel board story, preschoolers and school-age children should be given a chance to use the pieces themselves and retell the story. Ask each provider to leave his or her flannel piece on the table so that all participants can see them during break or for a few minutes following the workshop.

Homemade books are an excellent way to enrich the book selection in a family child care home. They might include books of photographs of the children themselves, stories about the children or ones they make up, or familiar fairy tales. When the pages are covered with clear contact paper, the books can be used by children of all ages. Collect some samples you can share with participants, and invite those who brought books to share them with the group. If participants are interested, time could be scheduled to make books for their programs at a later date.

Activity VI: Storytelling

In a short presentation, discuss the following points about storytelling:

- Some people have a gift for telling stories.

- Storytelling experiences open up a new world for many children, especially those who need more eye-to-eye contact and a more animated style to keep their attention.

- Encouraging children to tell stories themselves builds important skills for reading.

- When children are encouraged to tell an original story or retell one they know, their language tends to be animated and expressive.

- Children often begin their stories with "once upon a time," specify a place and time where the action takes place, describe one or more characters, and include a sequence of events.

Providers can encourage children to make up stories by asking leading questions such as these:

- Who is in your story?
- Where is this person?
- What happened first?
- Then what happened?
- How did he react to that?
- What happened at the end?

Children also enjoy working up a group story where everyone adds part of the story. This encourages both imagination and language development while fostering socialization skills.

If possible, tape a group story done by children and play it for the class. If this is not possible, consider asking the participants if they would like to join you in making up a group story. Begin with an opening such as the following:

"It was a cold and windy day in the darkest part of winter. As I walked toward my house, I saw the biggest...." Point to the first participant. That person adds to the story and points to the next person until everyone has had a turn.

Activity VII: Sharing Books with Parents

Lead a discussion on how parents can be involved in experiences related to books. Some ideas you can add to this discussion include the following:

- donating used books;
- helping to make original books;
- borrowing books from the library; and
- coming in to read or tell stories to the children.

Conclusion

Summarize what was shared during this workshop, noting that many good ideas on selecting and using books were offered and emphasizing the importance of books to children.

Sand and Water

Purpose of the workshop:

To encourage family child care providers to include sand and water activities in their program.

In this workshop, participants will:

- explore the properties of sand and water and experience the benefits of adding props;
- exchange ideas for including sand and water activities in their programs;
- discuss barriers to successful sand and water play;
- plan an activity that incorporates sand or water play into their programs; and
- discuss methods of involving parents.

Materials you will need:

- flip chart, stand, and markers;

- individual or large plastic tubs for water and for sand;

- warm and cold water;

- fine and course sand;

- food coloring;

- liquid dishwashing detergent;

- sawdust, rice, beans, or oatmeal;

- props for sand and water play (e.g., containers, plastic tubing, egg beaters, bulb syringes, small paintbrushes, medicine droppers, corks, ping-pong balls, troughs, cookie cutters, sieves, colanders);

- a homemade balance scale (made with bread scraps, margarine tubs, and string);

- straws, pipe cleaners, plastic heavy baskets;

- frames to make bubble blowers (wire frames, straws, pipe cleaners, plastic berry baskets, etc.); and

- clean-up materials, including brooms, mops, sponges, paper towels, and dust pans.

What providers should bring:

- a prop they use for sand and water play

- sample smocks or aprons.

Introducing the Workshop

- Talk about the fact that sand and water are soothing materials that appeal to children's love of sensory experiences and that in using these natural materials, children become scientists and mathematicians.

- Emphasize that sand and water play are key elements in high-quality infant and toddler care.

- Discuss what you plan to cover in the workshop and your goals.

Activity I: Your Own Experiences with Sand and Water

Ask participants to become as comfortable as possible and then to shut their eyes. Tell them to take 5 deep breaths, try to clear their minds of any thoughts, and just relax. Ask them to recall a time in their childhood (or a more recent experience, if they prefer) when they played with sand and water. Have them picture this time in their minds. Then pose the following questions:

- Who were you with?

- What did the sand and/or water feel like? Hot, cold, wet, slippery, soft?

- Was it fun? Why?

- How did you feel? Exhilarated? Happy? Relaxed?

- How did it smell? Sound? Taste?

Suggest that participants stay with their image as long as they like and open their eyes when they feel ready. Invite participants to share what they remember. If appropriate, share your own memories of playing with sand and water. There will probably be a wide range of experiences in the group. They may include some of the following:

Running through the hose
Playing in the bathtub or sink
Playing in the water while doing dishes
Splashing in mud puddles
Blowing bubbles
Being squirted by the hose or fire hydrant
Making a fort of sand
Playing at a lake or in the ocean

Point out how these memorable experiences give us an idea of why sand and water activities are enjoyable for children.

Refer participants to the section in the Curriculum on helping children learn through sand and water play. If most people's memories were of experiences from older ages, be sure to direct the discussion to ihclude the benefits of sand and water play for infants and toddlers.

Activity II: Exploring Sand and Water

The introduction of this activity to the group is an important element of its success. Explain to the participants that you have set up sand and water play as they might in their homes. In this activity, participants will have an opportunity to explore sand and water themselves so that they will be more comfortable offering them to children.

Before the session begins, set up the sand and water basins. Place warm water in one and cold water in another. Next to each basin, place food coloring and liquid soap. In the sand basin, place both fine and coarse sand, if possible. (You can also provide additional bins with rice, beans, uncooked oatmeal, and sawdust for comparison.) Have clean-up supplies on hand to demonstrate ways to include children in clean-up activities, and use plastic under the table and smocks or aprons for the participants, just as providers might do at home.

Invite participants to play with the water first. Give the following instructions:

- Start with just plain water and see what you can do with it.

- Now, add the liquid soap and/or food coloring and see what happens.

Ask questions that encourage participants to think about their experience and discoveries.

- How does water sound? Feel? Look?

- Does water have a temperature?

- What happened when you added soap? Food coloring? How did the water change?

Encourage the participants to talk among themselves about what is happening. You may hear comments such as the following:
- Water sounds hard when you slap it.
- Water whooshes.
- Water seems quiet/fast/slow.
- Water is clear/cloudy/plain/soapy.
- Bubbles tickle.
- Bubbles fly/burst/explode.
- Water makes waves.

Watch the group for clues as to when it is time to move on. Usually, this part of the activity will take only a few minutes.

To summarize the experience, note that exploration with water by itself enables children to discover its many properties, but it is limited. When props are added, children can experiment even more.

Next, invite participants to explore the different types of sand provided (and to compare them with the other substances, if any). Ask questions to encourage participants to talk about what they are experiencing:

- How does sand feel? Look?

- How does your experience change when using coarse sand?

- How many different ways can you use sand?

- How does sand differ from the other substances? Are they alike in any ways?

You might hear comments such as the following:
- Sand is cool/warm.
- Sand is soft/grainy/coarse.
- Wet sand feels heavier than dry sand.
- Sand can be piled up.
- Set sand can be poked and molded.
- Sand is quiet.
- You can't see through sand.
- Sawdust is fine like sand.
- Rice and beans don't stick to your hands, and they are noisier.

To summarize the experience, note that children enjoy both fine and coarse sand. Coarse sand is easier to mold when wet; fine sand works well with sifters and colanders. Point out that we can sometimes offer children other substances in place of sand because they provide a different experience and are often easier to clean up.

Remind participants that infants, toddlers, and school-agers will enjoy and learn from these experiences just as much as preschoolers do. Challenge participants to keep thinking about the benefits for children of all ages.

Activity III: Using Props to Stimulate Sand and Water Play

Display on the table the props you have collected for the session, and invite participants to select the ones they want. Allow 10 to 15 minutes for participants to experiment with the props in sand and water. Ask them to consider the following:

- Which props work best with sand?

- What do you think children would do with these props?

- What skills and concepts might they learn when using these props with sand and water?

Point out that water and sand alone will not maintain children's interest for long. When a variety of interesting props are added, children will continue to explore sand and water, learning many concepts in the process.

Next, form 3 work groups and assign each group one of the following tasks:

1. Create a dramatic play scene for the sand table. (Provide small cardboard boxes, twigs, seashells, plastic animals, small trucks and cars, pipe cleaners, popsicle sticks, and so on.)

2. Create a variety of bubble blowers. (Provide pipe cleaners, wire bubble frames, straws, funnels, bubble pipes, plastic berry baskets, and bubble soap.) How many different sizes and shapes of bubbles can you make with your blowers?

3. Think of a variety of weighing activities. (Provide either a ready-made scale or a homemade balance scale with various types of containers for sand and water, such as styrofoam cups, margarine containers, paper plates, or yogurt containers.)

Allow approximately 15 minutes for this activity. Have each group talk about what it did and how to apply what was learned to the family child care program.

Activity IV: Barriers to Sand and Water Play and How to Overcome Them

Present this next topic by stating that many providers avoid sand and water play because they see too many problems in doing it easily and effectively. Lead a brainstorming session by posing the following situation:

Suppose you didn't want to include sand and water activities in your program. Brainstorm all the reasons and examples you could give me for not offering sand and water activities as part of your program.

List all the ideas on one side of a chart. They may include some of the following:

- It's too messy indoors.
- Children get sand in their eyes and hair.
- It's not easy to supervise infants.
- Children get wet.
- No one wants to clean up.
- I can't supervise children in the bathroom.
- It's not interesting for school-age children.
- I don't have enough props.
- I don't know where to get sand.

Divide participants into small groups and assign each group an equal number of barriers. Have the groups identify at least 2 ways of overcoming each barrier. When you reconvene the groups, invite them to share their ideas.

Activity V: Planning for Sand and Water Activities

Ask participants to find a partner and discuss the ideas for sand and water play that they have learned today. Have each pair decide on one activity to incorporate into its program. Ask each pair to write down a plan. The plan should include:

- what materials the partners will need;
- where they can get the materials;
- where the activity can be done;
- how they will involve children of different ages; and
- how parents can be involved.

Suggest that partners exchange phone numbers and call each other to see how the activity went. If you will meet with this same group of providers, have them report back at the beginning of the next session.

Activity VI: Sharing Sand and Water with Parents

Parents can support sand and water activities—and even overlook the inconvenience of a little sand in their child's shoes or hair—if they understand the value of sand and water play. Ask participants what kind of support they would like to receive from parents:

- How could parents help you in offering sand and water play activities?

- How could you use the letter on sand and water in the *Curriculum* to make parents aware of the role they can play?

Conclusion

Acknowledge that offering sand and water experiences requires planning and preparation but is often worth the effort. Encourage participants to try out some of the ideas you have discussed, and remind them to call their partners.

Cooking

Purpose of the workshop:

To show how cooking experiences can be incorporated easily into a family child care program and how children of all ages can be involved.

In this workshop, participants will:

- think about what food means to them;

- try out and then share sample recipes;

- share ways of extending learning through cooking activities; and

- discuss ideas for involving parents in cooking activities.

Materials you will need:

- index cards with the names of different foods written on them (see Activity I);

- ingredients and utensils for 4 food experiences using your favorite recipes or the sample recipes included in this *Guide*; and

- recipe cards for participants.

What providers should bring:

- recipes they have used successfully with children.

Introducing the Workshop

- Talk about food experiences as a natural part of a family child care program and also as an important part of a curriculum.

- Review your goals for the workshop and what you plan to do.

Activity I: What Food Means to Me

Explain that the workshop will focus on cooking and food experiences for children of all ages. Tell participants that you are going to start by playing a game that will emphasize that each of us relates a variety of experiences and feelings with different foods.

Prior to the meeting, prepare index cards with the names of various foods written on them: turkey, pizza, chocolate chip cookies, tacos, greens, ham hocks, pie, peanut butter and jelly sandwiches, tomato soup, fried rice, or others. Be sure to include foods that are culturally and ethnically familiar to the participants.

Pass out the cards, one to each person, until they are gone. Ask for a volunteer to start by reading the name of the food from the card. The person to his or her right will then call out something he or she associates with that food. Encourage participants to get comfortable and have fun with this game.

Next, have participants randomly call out foods they hate and briefly share stories connected with those foods. You may hear such statements as these:

- I was forced to stay at the table and eat squash.
- I fed lima beans to my dog under the table.
- I hid peas under my mashed potatoes.

Bring the game to a close by pointing out that we all have strong feelings and memories associated with foods.

Facilitate a discussion on how our own experiences affect how we deal with food in a family child care home. Point out that in our society, food means many things in addition to nutrition. It often represents security, traditions, socializing, and celebrations.

Activity II: Trying Out a Recipe

Advertise this workshop as a dinner meeting so that participants will come prepared to eat a meal. Explain that they will be trying out recipes and evaluating them for use with children and that they will share a meal together.

Have food exploration stations already set up with ingredients, utensils, and recipe cards. Ask participants to select one of the stations so the work groups are evenly divided. Explain that they will use the recipe card and practice a cooking activity. When they are finished, give each group a card with the following questions to discuss over dinner.

> Would this be a good activity for children?
>
> What should providers think about if they want to do this activity (e.g., utensils, safety, place to do it)?
>
> Can children of all ages be involved in it? How?
>
> If it is not appropriate for all ages, when or how can it be done in the family child care setting?

After each group has completed its recipe, enjoyed the food, cleaned up, and answered the questions, invite each group to share its cooking experience with other groups. Have additional copies of the recipes so everyone can have a complete set to take home.

Activity III: Learning Through Food Experiences

Refer participants to the section on special activities in cooking in the chapter on Cooking. Ask them to think of ideas for improving the recipe they brought, or extending the learning resulting from the recipe. For example, if they brought a pudding recipe, they could tell children stories about where milk comes from or visit a farm and then, on another day, make butter from cream.

Invite participants to share their recipes with the group and describe how they have worked in their program. If possible, offer to make copies of the recipes for each person. If not, have everyone place their recipes on a table. Provide blank file cards and paper so people can copy the recipes they like.

Activity IV: Sharing Cooking Activities with Parents

Ask each person to think of one way to share information about cooking or to involve parents in cooking activities. Invite participants to briefly describe their idea and how it could be implemented. Ideas may include:

- making a recipe book for parents;
- inviting parents to come in and prepare a favorite dish with the children;
- asking parents about their child's favorite food;
- asking parents to send a favorite recipe;
- getting flyers on nutrition from the extension agency and giving them to parents;
- posting the daily food plan on a bulletin board; and
- borrowing cooking supplies from parents (e.g., grills, cookie cutters, and so on).

Conclusion

As a way of concluding this workshop, you may want to share the portion of the video *Caring and Learning* that shows the children making pizza.

Handout #6

Recipes*

AMAZING TRAIL MIX

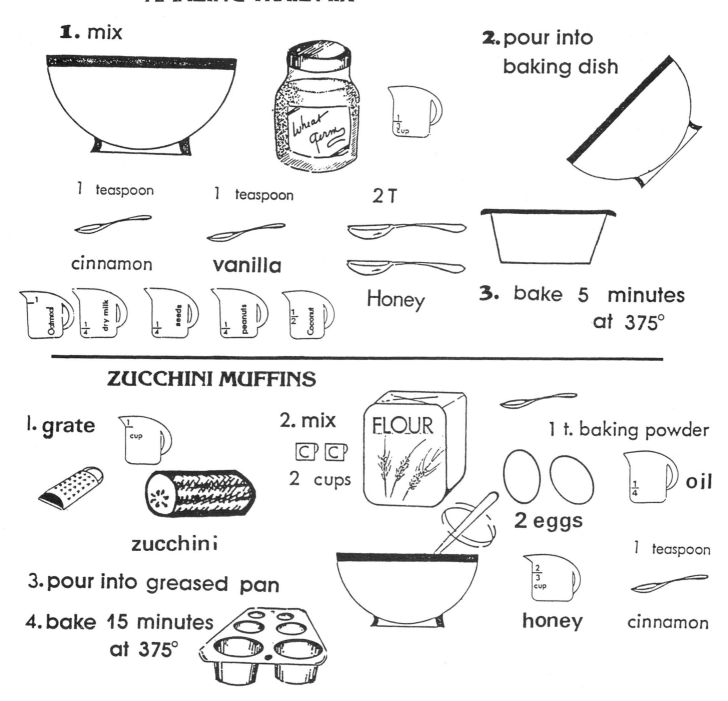

1. mix

1 teaspoon cinnamon

1 teaspoon vanilla

2 T Honey

Oatmeal

1/4 dry milk

1/4 seeds

1/4 peanuts

1/2 Coconut

2. pour into baking dish

3. bake 5 minutes at 375°

ZUCCHINI MUFFINS

1. grate

zucchini

2. mix

FLOUR

2 cups

1 t. baking powder

oil

2 eggs

2/3 cup honey

1 teaspoon cinnamon

3. pour into greased pan

4. bake 15 minutes at 375°

* **Note:** Reprinted from *Head Start Nutrition Education Curriculum* (U.S. Department of Health and Human Services, Office of Human Development Services, Administration for Children, Youth, and Families, Head Start Bureau, Washington, DC).

SPINNING WHEELS

1. remove crusts

2. spread peanut butter

3. peel

4. cut

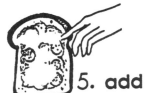

5. add

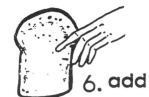

6. add

7. flatten

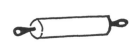

8. roll
and
cut

MUNCHING MIX

1. 2 cups
popcorn

2. add

½ cup
raisins

½ cup
peanuts

3. add

½ cup
peanut butter

4. mix

CUKE CANOES

1. peel

3. scoop out seeds

2. cut

4. spread peanut butter

5. top

TACO TWISTS

1. wash spinach

2. chop

3. grate cheese

4. brown beef   1 lb.

5. top

6. heat in oven 5 minutes

Music and Movement

Purpose of the workshop:

To introduce participants to a variety of creative ways to include music and movement activities in their daily program.

In this workshop, participants will:

- discuss how music and movement support children's development;

- share successful ways of involving children in music and movement activities;

- make instruments to use their programs; and

- discuss ways of involving parents in music and movement activities.

Materials you will need:

- a record player or cassette player;

- musical selections (preferably from the list in the *Curriculum*);

- index cards on which you have written the sample music and movement activities from the chapter on Music and Movement (Handout #7); and

- materials to make musical instruments (choose the ones you want participants to make from the chapter on Music and Movement).

What providers should bring:

- any materials they have at home to make instruments (send out a list of items prior to the workshop), and

- their favorite record or tape to use with children.

Introducing the Workshop

- Discuss how music and movement can be a part of every day in family child care and how they can brighten even a dreary and rainy afternoon.

- Review what you plan to do in the workshop.

Activity I: How Music and Movement Support Children's Development

Explain to participants that the purpose of this activity is to inspire them to think about how music and movement activities promote children's development. Introduce the notion that music and movement offer valuable learning opportunities in all developmental areas.

In either one large group or several smaller groups, have the participants discuss the statements previously prepared on index cards. Have them analyze which area of development the activity listed supports. Provide charts with the 4 areas of development (cognitive, social, emotional, and physical) blocked off, along with masking tape so that participants can secure the slips to the paper.

When they are finished taping on all the strips, facilitate a discussion about the activity. Be sure to ask if there were any disagreements about which category to put an activity in or if anyone wanted to place an activity in more than one category.

Ask providers to think about and discuss what age groups are represented by this sampling of activities.

Activity II: Music and Movement Activities That Work

Invite 3 or 4 experienced providers to act as a panel and present information on how they incorporate music and movement into their family child care settings. Ask the panel members to include what activities are done, at what time of day, what their favorites are, and how all the children are involved in the movement activities. If time permits, have each panel member teach a finger play and/or song to the group. Be sure to allot time for practicing so that workshop participants really learn them.

When the presentation is finished and providers have had a chance to ask questions, ask the participants to pair off and review the section in the *Curriculum* on helping children learn through music and movement. Have them look for additional ideas or methods of incorporating music and movement into their day.

Reconvene the group and ask each pair of participants to pick the 2 ideas they like the most from either the panel or the *Curriculum* and share them with the group. This should give everyone a chance to review the material and have some new ideas to try out.

Activity III: Make It, Take It, and Use It Tomorrow

Set out tables with sample homemade instruments, a copy of the instructions from the *Curriculum*, and the materials participants will need to make their own instruments. Discuss each of the instruments and how they were made. Encourage participants to make as many instruments as they want.

As the group is working, invite each person to share a favorite record or tape by playing it for the group. When everyone has made an instrument, play a lively piece and invite everyone to play their instruments.

Activity IV: Managing Children with Music and Movement

Discuss with providers the idea that music and movement can be used to manage children. Soft music soothes; dancing releases energy; group music encourages a feeling of group closeness; playing an instrument builds confidence; and so on.

Ask providers to give personal examples of times when music and movement has played a significant role in their home. As an alternative or in addition to these stories, read the story in the *Curriculum* about involving children of different ages.

Activity V: How to Involve Parents

One way that parents can participate in music and movement activities is by sharing their own special talents with the children. Ask if anyone has successfully involved parents in music activities. Discuss ways that providers can involve parents in music and movement activities. Some ideas may include the following:

- posting a copy of recommended books and records from the *Curriculum;*

- having the children make instruments during the day and take them home;

- asking parents to bring in favorite records or tapes;

- inviting parents who play an instrument to share it with the children; and

- playing favorite selections of music at drop-off or pick-up times.

Conclusion

Review some of the ideas presented during this workshop and play some music as participants gather their materials to take home.

Handout #7
Music and Movement Activities

(Write the following activities on index cards.)

- Turning toward a musical mobile while resting in a crib

- Banging a pan with a wooden spoon and saying "I make noise!"

- Making different sounds with musical instruments and recognizing differences in volume, tempo, and tone

- Replicating the sound of a drum beat on a record by beating on the bottom of a pan

- Learning how to shake maracas or bang a xylophone to produce musical sounds

- Playing "Ring Around the Rosey"

- Dancing together

- Reacting in different ways to music and sound

- Beginning to recognize favorite types of music and experimenting with movement

- Imitating simple finger plays

- Hopping, swaying, and leaping during creative movement

- Clapping and stamping feet in time to music

Outdoor Play

Purpose of the workshop:

To show how the outdoor environment offers a wide range of learning opportunities for children.

In this workshop, participants will:

• explore their own attitudes toward the use of the outdoor environment;

• identify barriers and solutions to taking children outdoors;

• explore learning opportunities outdoors;

• look at ways of using the outdoors creatively;

• discuss the value of outdoor play for all areas of development; and

• brainstorm ideas for involving parents.

Materials you will need:

• a flip chart and paper;

• paper and markers; and

• large paper bags.

What providers should bring:

• a play material they use outdoors for infants, toddlers, preschoolers, and school-age children.

Introducing the Workshop

- Discuss the value of the outdoors as a rich environment in which children can explore and learn.

- Acknowledge that it's not always easy to take a group outdoors.

- Review your goals and what you plan to do in the workshop.

Activity I: Attitudes Toward the Outdoors

Ask participants to think back to when they were children and played outdoors. Pose these questions:

- Where did you like best to play?

- What were you doing?

- How did it feel to be in that space?

- What did it smell like?

Often people recall experiences such as the following:

- playing in dirt (or mud, water, or sand) when I was a child;

- riding bicycles with a friend;

- finding a secret and quiet place to be alone and think;

- walking outside in the summer after it rained and splashing through puddles; and

- collecting things such as acorns, shells, bugs, and leaves.

Then ask participants to visualize themselves as an older or younger child and imagine an outdoor experience. Note if there are any changes to the list previous generated.

Point out how these experiences differ from the ones children have indoors. Stress that if we avoid taking children outdoors, we miss many valuable learning opportunities.

Activity II: Overcoming Barriers to Using the Outdoors

Providers face typical problems that may prevent them from using the outdoors effectively. Finding realistic solutions to these problems can help providers use and enjoy the outdoors more.

Brainstorm as a group about all the problems or barriers that get in the way of making the outdoors a rich environment for learning. Then form small groups and ask each to identify solutions to the problems. Reconvene the entire group to hear reports on solutions identified. As each small group reports, note its ideas on the flip chart. Refer participants to the section on logistics in the chapter on Outdoor Play for additional ideas.

BARRIERS	SOLUTIONS
The outdoors is too cold.	Wear appropriate clothing. Keep active outdoors. Keep extra mittens and hats for children.
There's not enough time.	Schedule outdoor time as part of the daily program. Allow sufficient time for children to put on coats and other accessories and to take them off.
It takes the little ones too long to get dressed and undressed.	Allow extra time so children can practice self-help skills. Ask older children to help the younger ones.
There's not enough to do outdoors.	Bring some indoor activities outside each day. Learn group games you can play. Identify places nearby that offer variety.
I don't have a yard.	Use a nearby park. Take walks around the block. Team up with another provider nearby and use her yard or go together to parks.
It's hard to supervise the children.	Use playpens for infants and toddlers. Ask older children to help. Busy children are easier to supervise—plan lots to do.

Activity III: Exploring Learning Opportunities Outdoors

The following activity will give participants a chance to identify some of the many learning opportunities available outdoors. Ask participants to select a partner for a short walk through the playground or the surrounding neighborhood. Urge each pair to think in terms of what they hope children would notice, or what they might point out if a child was with them. Give each person a paper bag so he or she can collect any interesting items during the walk. Ask participants to look for and collect things that will help children develop the following:

- an understanding of and interest in the outdoor environment and
- skills in sorting and classifying.

When the group returns, encourage people to share the experience and what they found. List their discoveries on the flip chart. Here are some examples of what you might hear:

- For an understanding of the outdoor environment:

    rain water evaporating
    buds appearing on the trees
    worms under a rock
    clouds moving in the sky

- For classification skills:

    rock collections to sort
    leaves of different sizes and shapes
    acorns, chestnuts, and other seeds
    trash

Summarize the exercise by making the following points:

- Outdoors, children have unique opportunities to observe nature firsthand, to explore, and to enjoy the freedom of space and movement.

- The outdoors is an evolving learning environment. It contains many raw materials such as grass, dirt, and water that are naturally appealing to young children. The environment changes with the seasons, providing new learning opportunities.

Activity IV: Using the Outdoors Creatively

Point out that one way to extend the use of the outdoor environment is to find creative and imaginative ways to use what's available. Divide participants into 4 groups and assign each group one of the following tasks. Direct participants to review the chapter on Outdoor Play for ideas. Here are some questions to ask:

- Design 2 water play experiences that could take place outdoors. What props would you need? How would you set up these experiences?

- How many different things do you think children could do with hoops, balls, and rope? What would infants do? Toddlers? Preschoolers? School-age children?

- How many different ways could you use cardboard cartons as play materials outdoors?

- If you had nothing but an open, grassy area for outdoor play, what could you bring outdoors to create an interesting environment?

Allow approximately 15 minutes for this activity and then have each group report. Make handouts from the information presented and mail them to the participants, or give them out at the next session. Emphasize the following points:

- Providers can create an interesting outdoor environment by giving children props they need for play.

- Any outdoor space that you have available can be used creatively with a little planning.

- The outdoor environment naturally changes throughout the year. This provides even more opportunities to create an exciting learning environment.

Activity V: The Outdoors and All Areas of Development

Ask providers to reflect on the information presented thus far in the workshop.

Place 4 sheets of paper on the wall with markers nearby, each labeled with an area of development: cognitive, social, emotional, or physical. Ask providers to move from sheet to sheet (individually or in small groups) and list ways that outdoor play can enhance development in each area.

Announce that they should move on to a new area every 3 minutes or so until everyone has had an opportunity to record an idea in each area.

Reconvene the entire group and suggest that everyone look over the charts and point out any ways of development that are of particular interest to them.

Activity VI: Sharing the Outdoors with Parents

It's important for parents to understand why outdoor play is part of the daily program and how it contributes to their children's development. Refer participants to the letter on outdoor play. Ask questions such as the following to generate a discussion:

- How could you use this letter to help parents understand this aspect of your program?

- What support do you need from parents?

- What are some ways in which you can obtain cooperation from parents?

Conclusion

Briefly summarize the content of this workshop and challenge the participants to find additional things of interest outdoors. (Ask about these at the next session if you will be working with this group again.)

Building Partnerships with Parents

Purpose of the workshop:

To provide a forum for parents and providers to share concerns and identify strategies for working together in a partnership.

In this workshop, participants will:

- examine challenges that must be overcome in establishing an effective parent-provider partnership;

- consider case studies of parent-provider interactions;

- share ideas for communicating with parents and involving them in the program and its curriculum; and

- celebrate the importance of working together.

Preparation for the workshop:

Prior to the workshop, talk with providers about the idea of inviting parents to join the group for a session on building partnerships with parents. Ask providers for suggestions of parents to invite to this session. Contact each parent and explain the goals of the workshop. Ask them to be thinking about information they want from their provider and what communication methods they find most effective.

If you have already presented workshops on many of the topics in the *Curriculum,* you might encourage providers to work together in teams to plan mini-presentations for parents on some of their favorite activities.

Materials you will need:

- a bag of assorted objects (see the list in the introductory workshop);

- name tags;

- index cards and pencils; and

- refreshments for a celebration at the end of the workshop (each person could bring a dish).

What providers should bring:

- samples of communications they give to parents (e.g., information sheets, policies, contracts, letters, workshops, invitations);

- any materials they will need for their mini-workshops; and

- a dish for the celebration.

Introductory Activity: Something About Me

Welcome all participants and give a special welcome to the parents who have come. Explain that in working with young children, we all recognize how important it is for them to have real objects and materials to play with. Tell the participants that in keeping with that idea, you are going to play an introductory game using real objects. Then pass around the bag of objects and ask each person to take one.

Instruct participants to examine their object carefully, get to know it, take it for a walk around the room if they like, and play with it. Think about how the object is like them and how it is different. Explain that in 3 minutes you will ask participants to introduce themselves and their object and state how they are like and different from their object.

Activity I: Questions I've Always Wanted to Ask

Form 2 groups, 1 of parents and 1 of providers. Give each a set of index cards and pencils. Explain that this is their opportunity to ask the questions they've always wanted to ask but have been uneasy about bringing up. No names will be used on the cards.

Allow about 5 minutes for parents and providers to write their questions. Then collect the cards and hand them to the opposite group. Ask each group to review the questions they have received and discuss how they might respond. If time permits, suggest that each group try to explain why a particular issue would be hard to bring up. Have each group select a spokesperson who will present its responses.

Activity II: Case Studies

In this activity, providers and parents will be working together to discuss sample situations and how they should be resolved. Form 3 small groups and give each one a situation card. Ask participants to select a recorder who will be responsible for taking notes and presenting their ideas at the end. Allow approximately 10 to 15 minutes for the discussions.

Situation # 1

Mr. and Mrs. Smith have a toddler in Ms. Jarvis's family child care program. On several occasions when the Smiths arrived to pick up their child, Ms. Jarvis was at the park instead of at home. The Smiths had to wait outside until the group returned before they could pick up their child. This was a great inconvenience for them, and they were annoyed.

How should the parents handle the situation?
What might the provider do?

Situation #2

Ms. Ford worked for 5 years as a teacher in a child care center. When her own child was born, she decided to stay home and run a family child care program. She cares for a toddler, 2 preschoolers, and a school-age child in addition to her own infant. She loves what she is doing and feels that the program she provides meets the same standards as the one she offered at the center. However, her relationships with parents are quite different. Now that she is a family child care provider, the parents treat Ms. Ford as a babysitter, not a professional caregiver, and they think they have a right to dictate what the program should be like. Ms. Ford is so discouraged by this lack of respect that she is thinking of ending her program.

What should Ms. Ford do to improve her relationships with the parents?
What would help the parents acknowledge Ms. Ford's professionalism?
What could parents do to address Ms. Ford's feelings, assuming they are aware of those feelings?

Situation #3

Mr. Dunning has two children in Ms. Ortega's program, a toddler and a 3-year-old. On cold days Mr. Dunning tells the provider that he wants the children to stay inside because they get too cold and he doesn't want them to be sick. Outdoor time is an important part of Ms. Ortega's program. She feels that being outdoors is healthy for children, and she plans for this time as she does for her indoor activities.

How should Ms. Ortega handle the situation?
What would help Mr. Dunning accept outdoor time for his children?
What would help Ms. Ortega meet the needs and concerns of this parent?

Situation #4

Mr. Drew has repeatedly asked for a payment receipt from the family child care provider who cares for his 2 children. He needs to submit this to his employer every month in order to receive child care credits. The provider, Ms. Lee, promises to have the receipts ready the next day but regularly forgets.

What should Mr. Drew do to get the payment receipts he needs?
What might help Ms. Lee respond more positively?

After about 10 or 15 minutes minutes, find out from each group if it needs more time. When everyone appears to be finished, have the recorders report on their discussions and solutions.

Activity III: Why We Use a Curriculum for Family Child Care

This activity gives providers a chance to share parts of the *Creative Curriculum* with parents by presenting some of the activities they have experienced in previous workshops. You might begin the workshop by showing the *Curriculum* to the parents and explaining the role of a curriculum in family child care (see the first workshop). Introduce each of the provider groups and explain what part of the *Curriculum* they will be presenting.

Activity IV: Ideas That Work

Invite participants to share some of the communication methods they feel work best in supporting the parent-provider partnership. Both providers and parents may have materials and ideas to share.

Activity V: A Celebration

Thank all the parents who participated in the workshop and the providers who made presentations. Acknowledge that good relationships take work but that children benefit the most when their parents and providers are working together to support them. Congratulate the providers for the commitment to high-quality child care that is evident in their attendance at these professional workshops. Invite everyone to enjoy the celebration.

Conclusion

In this chapter we've presented a number of ideas for workshops that we hope you'll be able to use in training family child care providers. Through workshops such as these, you can introduce providers to *The Creative Curriculum for Family Child Care* and motivate them to implement the *Curriculum* in their daily work with children.

III. Working on Setting the Stage with Providers in Their Homes

One of your most important tasks as a trainer or supervisor of family child care providers is to ensure that *The Creative Curriculum for Family Child Care* is being used as intended. Primarily, this means that the *Curriculum* is being applied in developmentally appropriate ways and that the home environment supports learning. Although developmentally appropriate care should be a cornerstone of all caregiving programs, it is especially vital for family child care programs because these programs typically serve children of varying ages and skill levels.

In this chapter we will explore ways in which you can assess how effectively providers have set up their homes so that the *Creative Curriculum* can be implemented successfully. The topics addressed in this chapter refer to guidance that providers will have received in Setting the Stage.[2]

Environment

When you walk into an effective family child care home, you should be struck by two things: the provider has arranged the home to facilitate children's growth and development, and the environment has retained the warm, cozy atmosphere of a home. An effective environment for family child care is one in which the rooms in the home have been arranged to include spaces for children's play, for storing play materials in easy reach of the children, for displaying children's work, and for storing children's personal items. In setting up the home, the provider should also maintain aspects of the home that provide children with security and comfort: sofas, rocking chairs, cushions, and personal items used by family members of all ages. Listed below are examples of what you will see in a home in which the *Creative Curriculum* is being implemented effectively.

What You Should See	Why
Furnishings are appropriate to the ages of the children being cared for. For example, cribs, high chairs, and changing tables are available for infants; booster chairs for toddlers; and child-sized tables and chairs for toddlers, preschoolers, and school-age children.	If providers care for children of varied ages, there should be a variety of furnishings to meet the needs of all the children in the home. Children need safe, comfortable furnishings that will allow them to master their environment. Child-sized tables and chairs, for example, make it easier for a child to eat a meal or concentrate on finger painting.

---

[2]Much of the content in this chapter is taken from materials previously written by the authors in *A Handbook for Army Education Program Specialists*, U.S. Department of the Army, Washington, DC, 1989.

What You Should See

Why

Sufficient space in the home is made available to children so that they can actively play, take naps, and eat meals.

Young children need space to move about if they are to grow and develop fully. Providers who confine children to a small bedroom might be protecting their home from wear and tear, but they are also neglecting children's needs.

The home is arranged so that children understand which areas they can use and which are out of bounds.

To be free to explore their environment, children need to know which spaces are theirs for the day. Clear boundaries help children learn to respect the rules of the home.

Areas of the home that are out of bounds to the children are blocked off by a door, a gate, or a large piece of furniture. Objects that active children might break are kept in an out-of-bounds area.

When the physical arrangement of the home communicates to children what the limits are, the provider does not have to keep reminding children of where they are allowed to be. By making the out-of-bounds areas inaccessible to children, providers help children learn to respect rules. Removing breakable objects is just common sense; young children cannot be expected to leave breakable objects alone.

The home is child-proofed. For example, electrical outlets are covered, loose carpets are tacked down, plastic bags and household detergents are locked away, and stairways are protected; cribs are out of reach of venetian blind cords; and the paint on toys and walls is nontoxic.

All children need a safe, healthy environment. Child-proofing a home helps ensure children's safety and frees the provider from constantly safeguarding the children's every move.

Items to stimulate learning are displayed on walls. For example, mobiles are placed near cribs or changing tables, mirrors are hung at children's eye level, and photographs of field trips or children's special projects are posted for all to see.

Children learn from everything in their environment, including items and objects that are hung on walls. Carefully selected wall displays promote learning and stimulate discussion.

What You Should See

Spaces in the home are available to accommodate children's individual learning needs. For example, the home includes uncluttered floors—carpeted and uncarpeted—for infants to practice crawling and walking; quiet places for toddlers, preschoolers, and school-age children to look at books, do a puzzle, or be alone; and areas set aside for toddlers, preschoolers, and school-age children to engage in noisy activities such as playing with water, finger painting, or engaging in dramatic play.

An outdoor area or access to an outdoor play area is available for children's daily play. The outdoor area has spaces for sand and water play and gardening. Equipment for large muscle play (such as swings and climbing apparatus) is also included.

Why

Children need to have sufficient space, undisturbed by others, to work on projects, develop and practice skills, and participate in activities. To set the stage for growth and development, providers need to arrange their homes to meet the needs, skills, and interests of all the children in their care.

Children's growth and development is promoted by outdoor activities as well as indoor ones. By structuring the outdoor environment so that different types of activities can take place, providers can make the outdoors an exciting place for children.

When the Environment Is Not Working

In a family child care home like the one described above, the children will be busy and happily at play. If you see children standing around with nothing to do, children who cling to the provider, children who are fighting or screaming, or providers who seem unable to cope with the children in their care, it may be that the environment is inappropriate. The following section lists some warning signs that might indicate that a provider needs assistance in changing the components in the home setting to better support her or his caregiving efforts.

Warning Signs	Why This Might Be Happening	What You Might Do
Infants and older children constantly bump into each other or interfere with each other's activities.	Infants might not have a safe space for crawling or toddling, older children might not have areas large enough for moving about, or there might not be clear paths for moving around the play areas in the room.	Work with the provider to rearrange the environment so that children have space to move freely. Also, help the provider create pathways around all activity areas. You might try using a doll house or blueprint paper to help the provider "visualize" in advance what the home should look like.

Warning Signs	Why This Might Be Happening	What You Might Do
Children run around the house in circles, squealing excitedly.	The rooms in the home are probably laid out so that all the rooms connect. Once children discover this, they're off and running.	Work with the provider to restructure the layout so that a circular pathway is no longer available. This might be done by making a room out of bounds, moving a piece of furniture in front of a pass-through, or boxing in play areas with furnishings.
When inside on bad-weather days, children climb and jump on furniture.	The provider might allow children to run wild because they have had no opportunity to release their pent-up energy outdoors.	Work with the provider to incorporate indoor exercises such as dancing to music or calisthenics into the daily schedule. This will allow children to release their energy productively without creating chaos for everyone. Help the provider plan a space in the home where children can exercise or dance with abandon.
The home has been converted into a mini-center.	Some providers might believe that the best indication that they are providing high-quality care is that their home looks and operates like a school-based center.	Help the provider understand that the home should include some elements similar to those of a center but that family child care should be deliberately designed to look and operate differently.
Children with disabilities (if present) keep bumping into furniture, appear uncomfortable using the designated play spaces, or become frustrated because they don't have easy access to materials, toys, and books.	The provider might not have cared for children with disabilities before and has arranged the home in a way that has worked effectively in the past.	Children with special needs need special accommodations to the environment. Work with the provider to develop a layout that will meet the particular needs of each child with special needs cared for in the home. This might require moving furniture, making toys and materials more accessible, widening pass-throughs, or installing pullaway ramps.

Equipment and Materials

One of the hallmarks of developmentally appropriate care is the provision of materials and equipment that stimulate learning. In family child care this task is complicated because children can vary in age from young infants to school-agers. This means that a provider must have a wide range of toys and learning materials. The wider the range of ages served, the greater the variety of materials needed. A provider who has all infants or all preschoolers in her care will find it easier to equip her home than a provider who cares for children of many ages and stages. Similarly, a provider who cares for a handicapped or sick child will need to have materials that address the child's special needs. Thus, the task of selecting appropriate materials is one that many providers find difficult, especially because acquiring materials for many developmental levels can be expensive.

By working with providers using the guidance presented in Setting the Stage, you can help providers maintain an appropriate, safe inventory of toys and play equipment. The following are instances of what you should see in a family child care home using the *Creative Curriculum* effectively.

What You Should See	Why
Toys and equipment are in good repair and free of jagged edges, rust, dirt, peeling paint, or any other dangerous features.	Children's safety is the first concern of child care. The children should not have access to any toys or equipment that are even slightly damaged.
Children are using materials and equipment appropriate to their developmental stages. For example, infants use their senses to explore soft, cuddly toys; toddlers put together simple puzzles and pull toys across the room; preschoolers practice skills on self-help boards and a variety of dramatic play props; and school-age children read books, work on craft projects, and listen to music.	Children learn through using play materials that are of interest to them and that challenge their minds and bodies without frustrating them. An age-appropriate inventory of equipment and materials is the basis of a developmental program.
A changing inventory of materials reflects the children's growth and interests. (See Setting the Stage in Chapter II.)	Learning is dynamic in nature; it must be supported by materials that ensure its progress. As children grow and develop new interests, they need to use materials that continually challenge them. If they have no new toys or materials to explore, they will soon become bored. To capture teachable moments, providers can add props or books on subjects that become of interest to the children. For example, following the first snowfall, shovels, sleds, and igloo props might be introduced. Stories about snow adventures could be checked out of the library and cassettes such as *Frosty the Snowman* played on the tape recorder.
Children use materials that allow them a wide variety of experiences, including art, music, cooking, block play, dramatic play, outdoor play, sand and water play, books, and toys.	Children need exposure to a broad base of experiences if they are to develop cognitively, physically, socially, and emotionally. Exposure to many types of activities is a feature of developmentally appropriate care.

What You Should See	Why
Children use toys and materials by themselves. For example, toddlers and preschoolers take out props for dramatic play whenever they like; infants reach out for cuddle toys and rattles; and older children remove art materials from the storage bin.	Children's learning is enhanced when they can be responsible for their own learning. By giving children access to materials, providers encourage this process.
Materials are added to the family child care home to reflect social problems or crises in the children's lives.	Children going through difficult times need opportunities to deal with their anxieties, express their frustrations, and cope with their fears or anger. Children may be experiencing a death in the family, a parental divorce, the birth of a sibling, or a health crisis. The provider should have books to read to the children which address these appropriate situations. Children also need opportunities to engage in dramatic play and art activities to help them work through their anxieties.
Children play with toys and materials (such as dolls, books, and dramatic-play props) that reflect their own ethnic and cultural backgrounds as well as those of the community in which they live.	Children learn best when they can identify with the characters in stories they read, the puppets they play with, and the people props they use for dramatic play and block adventures. When they see books and props that look like them, they regard these characters as role models and feel good about themselves. These materials also help children develop a respect for different ethnic groups and cultures.
Toys and materials are stored at the children's level and are easily accessible to them. Picture labels indicate where items are stored.	When children have access to play materials, they can make choices about what they want to do. This in turn helps them become self-motivated learners. Clean-up is also facilitated because children know where items are stored.

When Materials and Equipment Are Inappropriate

As you observe a family child care home, you will be able to tell rather easily if the provider has selected age-appropriate materials. If the home functions well and the children seem creative, busy, and happy, the materials are most likely appropriate. However, if you see frustrated, bored, or unhappy children, this might be due to inappropriate or insufficient materials and toys. Here are some warning signs you should look for and some suggested strategies for helping providers improve the equipment and materials in their homes.

Warning Signs	Why This Might Be Happening	What You Might Do
Very few toys and materials are available for children to play with. Those available are rarely changed.	Most providers understand the importance of play materials in stimulating children's learning. If few are present, the provider might have a limited budget for purchasing toys and equipment or might believe that with fewer materials, the home will become less messy.	Provide training on how to make homemade toys (such as blocks, puzzles, lotto games, and self-help boards). Encourage providers to establish a toy exchange. Work with providers to assemble rich (but not costly!) inventories of toys and equipment.
Children ignore the play materials, preferring to run around, push each other, or grab at the provider for attention.	Any number of reasons might be causing the children's behavior. For example, the materials might be too babyish or too advanced for the children; the toys and materials might be inaccessible to the children; or the provider might have established a schedule that allows only specific times for using using the materials.	Through careful observation and discussions with the provider, try to determine the cause of the problem. If the materials are inappropriate, help the provider see why these materials aren't working and suggest other toys that would be better suited to the children's needs. If the materials are inaccessible, work with the provider to create storage sites that are within the children's reach. If the provider has imposed time limits on using the materials, work with her or him to restructure the day so that children aren't left without anything to play with.
Children play with the same materials day after day in routine ways.	Children might be repeating actions to gain mastery over the material—which is part of learning. Alternatively, the children might be bored with the materials and not really paying attention to them.	Through direct observation you should be able to tell whether the children's repetition occurs thoughtfully or as a result of boredom. If it's the latter, work with the provider to make or secure materials that are slightly more complex and will therefore challenge the children.

Warning Signs	Why This Might Be Happening	What You Might Do
Children continually ask the provider how to complete a puzzle, draw a picture, or finish a project they've started.	The materials and toys might be too difficult for the children, or the children might need extra attention from the provider.	Observe the children to see what is taking place. If the materials or projects are too difficult for the children, work with the provider to make or secure toys that are better suited to the children's skill levels. If the children seem to need attention, discuss this with the provider and develop a plan she or he can follow to make the children feel more secure and confident.
Children fight over toys; everyone wants to play with the same thing at the same time.	There might not be enough variety in the materials and toys; the younger children might want to do what the older ones are doing; or the provider might not have provided enough duplicates of popular toys.	The first situation can be resolved by working with the provider to offer a more varied selection. The other situations, which are socio-developmental in nature, can be resolved through planning. Older children might be given activities to do while the younger children nap, thus avoiding conflict. Help the provider understand that most young children are not ready to share, and it is best to provide duplicates of popular items. Also, help the provider find materials that all children can enjoy—not just a few popular items.
Children tend to play with materials stereotypically— boys build with the blocks and girls cook and play house.	Children might be doing the activities they enjoy or might have received messages from adults that certain activities are only for boys and certain activities only for girls.	If children are engaged in stereotypical behavior because they enjoy it, there's no need to discourage them from playing this way just because we might feel it doesn't conform to what we'd like them to be doing. The provider can encourage children to try less stereotyped activities, but the children's own choice shouldn't be ignored. If, however, a provider is directly or indirectly giving children stereotypical messages about gender roles, you should discuss this with the provider.

Warning Signs	Why This Might Be Happening	What You Might Do
Toys and puzzles are stored in toy boxes. Children have to empty the box each time they want to use a particular toy.	The provider might think that toy boxes are good storage places because many children are already familiar with them. Or the provider might use toy boxes to save space.	Explain to the provider that while toy boxes might save space, they do not promote learning. Because toys must be stored haphazardly within the box, children become frustrated because they cannot readily find what they want. Also, because toys are usually just thrown in the toy box at clean-up time, children don't learn to sort and classify as they would if the toys were stored on labeled shelves.

Schedule and Routines

Scheduling in family child care must be tailored to meet the individual needs of the children being served. A home with infants, for example, must respond to the babies' individual eating and sleeping schedules. A mixed-age home has the even greater challenge of combining schedules for infants who need several naps with more active toddlers who need a little sleep and with preschoolers who are energy in action. A home with a handicapped or sick child might also have to customize the schedule to accommodate the child's health requirements. In addition, schedules must be flexible to reflect children's growth and changing interests. Scheduling therefore cannot be developed by an expert and duplicated in a family child care home. To truly work, it must be flexible enough to accommodate everyone's needs. Here's what you'll observe when a schedule is working well, allowing providers to implement *The Creative Curriculum for Family Child Care* effectively.

What You Should See	Why
Scheduled activities are appropriate for the developmental ages of the children served. Group activities are planned so that younger children can leave the activity when they become bored and older children can continue until they are finished.	Providers need to recognize that children's attention and interest in an activity increase with age. Thus, while group activities need to be long enough for preschoolers and school-age children to enjoy fully, they should be planned so that younger children can take a nap or go on to a new activity on their own. Children should be encouraged to participate in group activities only to the extent that they are interested and in capable of doing so.

What You Should See	**Why**
The schedule includes clean-up time.	Clean-up is a part of learning, and the schedule should include sufficient time for children to put away their playthings. This teaches children respect for their environment as well as themselves.
The schedule includes time for activities that are led by the provider and time for activities that are selected by the children.	Children need to make their own choices about what they want to play with. They also need the provider's guidance in reinforcing and extending their own play activities.
The schedule shows a balance between quiet and active times.	Children need times to express themselves actively and times to participate in quiet, soothing activities. Schedules need to accommodate children's natural energy levels.
The schedule is flexible enough to accommodate the unforeseen "teachable moment," such as a hailstorm, rainbow, or visitor.	A provider who rigidly follows a schedule is unable to take advantage of "teachable moments." By responding to the children's excitement when the snow starts falling, a provider can easily motivate children to learn.
The provider includes time in the daily schedule for talking and working with each child individually.	One of the unique benefits of family child care is that providers get to know each child as an individual and to nurture each child's growth in a loving way. Providers need schedules that are not so action-packed that they do not have time to relate to each child throughout the day. An infant who wakes up while children are building with blocks needs to be cuddled by the provider even as he or she is guiding the older children's efforts. Building in time for one-on-one interaction is crucial for good scheduling.

When the Program Schedule Is Not Working

If the daily schedule is not working well, it will most likely be obvious. A structure that breaks down is an invitation to frustration and chaotic behavior. Here are the signs that will tell you that the program schedule is not working as it should, along with some suggested strategies for helping providers develop schedules that will work.

Warning Signs	Why This Might Be Happening	What You Might Do
Children are wandering aimlessly without settling down with a toy or joining in an activity.	Several causes could be at work: activities might not be clearly scheduled during the day; children might not know what's expected of them; or the schedule might use blocks of time that are too long for the children's attention spans.	Work with the provider to develop a schedule that does not leave large blocks of time unaccounted for. Self-selected activity times, for example, can become overwhelming to children if they go on for a long time without some sort of direction.
The provider makes all the children participate in group projects such as painting a mural or making candles. Children who don't want to join in cry or disturb others. Infants crawl into the middle of the project, ruining everyone's time.	The provider might think that all the children, no matter what their ages, benefit from the group experience. Or the provider might find it easier to supervise children when they're all in one area of the room doing the same thing.	Acknowledge that all children might benefit from the group experience and that it is sometimes easier to supervise children when they are all together. However, work with the provider to show her why this approach is often not practical and sometimes not desired. Messy projects are usually best to initiate while infants nap. Children who don't want to should never be forced to participate "for their own good." Encourage providers who want the full group experience to offer activities that are likely to interest all the children, such as marching to music.
Lunch time goes on for hours, often taking up half the day.	The provider believes in letting children eat according to their own time clocks.	Help the provider understand that while infants should be fed on demand, no more than an hour of the day (usually around noon) should be set aside for a family-style lunch. The lunch hour is a time not just for eating but also for being together, sharing confidences, and enjoying each other's company. Even an infant who has just eaten can have a bottle of juice or water while the older children eat. This communal time is for many providers the highlight of the day. To keep it special, though, it should be limited to an hour from serving to clean-up.

Warning Signs	Why This Might Be Happening	What You Might Do
Children are too excited or wound up from play to take a nap.	The provider might believe in giving children lots of stimulation and sees this as a sign that the program is working.	Most children, including those of preschool-age, need to rest for a period. Help providers see nap time as an integral part of the day's activities. Infants should nap according to their individual time clocks; toddlers and preschoolers typically nap after lunch.
Children are all wound up at the end of the day, sometimes breaking into tears when they see their parents.	Children might be overtired because their naps were too short. The children might not be prepared for leaving because they just came in from an outdoor activity where they've been running around, or because they are involved in a favorite activity.	Help providers to better balance their daily plan so that children don't end up the day exhausted or at a high pitch and so that favorite activities are scheduled earlier in the day.
Children get into fights during group activities or play times.	The provider might not be managing activities, or the provider might not have enough materials for all the children to use during the group activity.	If the problem is insufficient materials, work with the provider on how to plan in advance for group activities. If the problem is one of management, help the provider structure the room arrangement to prevent problems.
The provider follows the schedule rigidly.	The provider might believe that the program is only as good as the schedule.	While planning is crucial, help the provider understand that a schedule that is not flexible is not suited to family child care. Children who want extra time to work on a block tower or to finish baking cookies need this time to feel they have accomplished their goals. A schedule that is too rigid to allow extra time or to accommodate the many teachable moments that occur during the day does not meet children's needs.

Warning Signs	Why This Might Be Happening	What You Might Do
Children follow a schedule that parallels almost exactly what goes on in a child care center.	The provider might believe that using a center-based schedule will ensure that the program is as developmentally appropriate as a program provided at a center.	Help the provider understand that while she or he can promote children's growth and development just as centers do, she or he does not have to turn the home into a mini-center. A high-quality family child home takes its scheduling cues from the children served. The ages and stages of the children are reflected in both the type and the sequence of the schedule.

Parent Involvement

The final element of Setting the Stage deals with how providers interact with parents. For the *Creative Curriculum* to be truly effective, parents need to be invested partners in the program. Here are some examples of what should be happening if a program is working well.

What You Should See	Why
An area of the family child care home is set up for sharing information with parents. For example, parents can leave a note for the provider on a sign-in sheet, leave a change of clothes for their children where the provider will find it, and pick up their children's take-home art, dirty clothes, and copies of the coming week's schedule and menus.	Communication between parents and providers is an essential element of high-quality child care. Communication is enhanced when a specific place is designated as a message center.
Providers greet parents by name as they drop off children in the morning and pick them up in the afternoon.	Social interaction of this sort conveys a message to parents that providers take an interest in them—and their children.
Providers communicate daily progress to parents.	Parents like to know how their children are faring each day. Successes as well as problems are important to parents.
Providers have on-file emergency phone numbers and medical information for each child.	Parents will be more secure knowing that providers know what to do should a medical or personal emergency arise.

What You Should See	**Why**
Providers regularly consult with parents for information on their children's favorite books, trips, foods, and so on.	Parents feel that their children and family are valued when providers attend to their children's preferences.
Providers regularly consult with parents when problem behaviors such as separation anxiety, biting or fighting arise.	When parents and providers join forces, a source for problem behaviors can usually be pinpointed. This makes resolving the problem relatively easy.
Providers share the *Creative Curriculum* with parents.	By letting parents know what their children are doing during the day, providers can enlist support for the program and the activities they're conducting.

Spotting Problems

While it's not always easy to detect a breakdown in parent-provider relationships, you can be on the alert for some obvious warning signals. Here are some things to look for:

- Parents drop off and pick up their children without stopping to chat with the provider beyond a cursory greeting.

- Parents' body language suggests coldness, formality, or irritation with the provider.

- There is no agreed-upon place for sharing information.

- Handouts prepared for parents by the provider are not picked up.

- Parents do not participate in workshops, meetings, or projects.

- The turnover rate at the family child care home is high.

If you suspect from your observations that parents are either indifferent or nonsupportive of a family child care home, action should be taken at once. You'll want to discuss the topic at length with the provider. In most cases the provider will be aware of the situation even if she or he is reluctant to admit it. Because parental nonsupport is looked upon negatively, take care not to accuse the provider or make her or him feel worse about an already precarious situation. Now is the time to take constructive action, not to focus on past mistakes. Together with the provider, analyze the situation and try to pinpoint problems. Are there personality problems? Do either parents or the provider feel intimidated by one another? Do parents not believe their involvement is appropriate? Do parents think their involvement would be unwelcome? Help the provider focus on the root(s) of the problem(s) so that a solution can be developed.

Once you've characterized the problem and its probable cause, the next step is to "make it go away." Together with the provider, develop an action plan for securing parent support. Include in this plan the steps the provider should take (e.g., scheduling a conference, sending out a newsletter, etc.), a timetable for seeing improvement, and signs that the provider can recognize as indications of improvement.

By working closely with providers in this area, you can help secure a strong bond between providers and parents. This partnership is crucial not just to the successful implementation of the *Creative Curriculum* but also for the total well-being of the children being cared for.

In this chapter we've explored topics related to Setting the Stage for learning. In the next chapter we'll examine how you can work with providers in their homes to implement Part Two, Activities, in the *Creative Curriculum*.

IV. Working on Activities with Providers in Their Homes

At the core of *The Creative Curriculum for Family Child Care* are the nine activity units. To help providers assess how effectively these units are being implemented, you will want to work one-on-one with them in examining their programs.

General Things To Look For

The *Creative Curriculum* functions both as individual activity units and as a total program. To determine if the program is working as it should be, your first step is to get a "feel" for what is happening in the provider's home. Are children actively engaged in activities, or do they seem bored or frustrated? Do children participate in a wide range of activities, or do they routinely do the same things each day? By taking a look at the program as a whole, you can get a sense of how well the *Curriculum* is working for both the provider and the children being served. Here are some things to consider in your observations.

What You Should See

Children participate in activities that are developmentally appropriate for their ages and stages.

Children participate in a wide variety of activities, such as building with blocks, engaging in dramatic play, shaking rattlers, turning pages of a book, writing letters, finger painting, making music, cooking, hammering nails into tree stumps, watering plants, and sifting sand through sieves.

Children participate in activities designed to promote cognitive development. For example, infants play peek-a-boo with older children; toddlers use simple shape sorters; preschoolers sort buttons; and school-age children work together on a jigsaw puzzle.

Why

Children learn best when the activities presented are challenging but not so advanced as to be overwhelming. In an effective family child care home, children are busily engaged in learning, not bored or frustrated.

Children learn through exposure to activities that tap all their senses and involve them in fun, innovative ways. A rich array of activities allows children to explore and appreciate their environment.

Children develop cognitive skills as they play with a rich variety of toys and materials. These activities help children develop skills and knowledge as well as a love for learning.

What You Should See	**Why**
Children participate in activities aimed at social/emotional growth. For example, infants watch and coo at the provider as she changes diapers; toddlers pretend they are doctors; preschoolers work together on a block structure; and school-age children plan a puppet show.	Children need to make sense of their world and to feel free to express their fears and anxieties in acceptable ways. These activities allow children to act out what is bothering them and develop greater confidence.
Children participate in activities that encourage the development of gross motor skills. For example, infants crawl, stretch, and pull up on furniture; toddlers and preschoolers jump, hop, and climb; and school-age children jump rope and do cartwheels.	Children thrive physically when they can use their bodies. They develop new gross motor skills when they have many opportunities to move about in their environment.
Children participate in activities aimed at the development of fine motor skills. For example, infants pick up pieces of food from their high chair trays; toddlers string large beads; preschoolers tear paper for collages; and school-age children sew puppets.	These kinds of activities help children develop and refine their fine motor skills. Children need to participate in increasingly difficult activities that improve their fine motor skills and eye-hand coordination.
Children take and return materials from the storage shelves.	Children learn best when given opportunities to be independent and take responsibility for their own learning.
Providers work one-on-one with children, asking them open-ended questions about what they are doing and encouraging children to try new things.	Providers who reinforce and extend children's learning by asking open-ended questions and suggesting strategies capture the essence of high-quality caregiving. Good providers take advantage of opportunities that arise to work individually with children.
Children participate in activities alone, in groups of two or three, or with the whole group.	Each type of experience is beneficial to children. Children need to be exposed to all three types of groupings over time to gain both intellectual and social growth.

What You Should See	**Why**
Older children help younger children.	One of the joys of family child care is the opportunity for tutoring by older children. In most instances, both sides will benefit. Younger children tend to prefer learning from a slightly older child, and older children like the ego gratification of showing a younger child how to do something they've already mastered. This is especially true when school-age children are in the home because toddlers and preschoolers tend to look up to these older youngsters.
Children with disabilities (if present) fully join in activities.	The home environment is ideally suited to including children with disabilities. Joining in the group experience enhances the confidence of the child with disabilities and conveys to all children a positive image of what people with disabilities can do (as opposed to what they cannot do).
Children participate in activities that take advantage of the home environment—both indoors and outdoors—such as sorting socks from the dryer, timing a hard-boiled egg, watering a plant, or feeding a pet.	As a general rule, activities should be an outgrowth of what occurs naturally in the home.

When the Program in General Is Not Functioning as It Should

If in your observations you find that the program does not seem to be working well, you will want to help the provider address the problems you've observed. The following warning signs indicate that the activities and learning experiences as a whole are not well suited to the children. Also included are suggested strategies for helping providers work on these problems.

Warning Signs	**Why This Might Be Happening**	**What You Might Do**
Activities led by the provider focus almost solely on intellectual growth (for example, singing alphabet songs, playing lotto games, matching pairs, using blocks to demonstrate geometry concepts, and conducting science experiments).	The provider might believe that cognitive development is more important than other kinds of development.	Discuss with providers the information presented in Setting the Stage, which explains why children need to participate in activities that will promote their physical and social/emotional growth as well as their cognitive development.

Warning Signs	Why This Might Be Happening	What You Might Do
Children choose to participate in the same activities day after day.	Children might like these activities so much that they keep at them day after day; they might be practicing skills that they are not yet comfortable with; they might not know what else there is to play with; or the other materials might be inaccessible to the children.	Observe the home to determine what is at the root of this behavior. If children are enjoying the activities or still experimenting, encourage the provider to reinforce the children's play and then to extend it gently. If children are repeating the same activities because they don't know what else there is to do, show the provider how to make other choices accessible to the children.
Almost all activities are group ones.	The provider might believe that children learn best from group experiences or that supervision is less of a hassle when all the children are together in one place.	While you don't want to discourage providers from doing group activities with all the children, point out to the provider that children also need the experience of playing in groups of two or three, playing alone, and playing together with the provider. An effective program needs a balance of approaches.
A child with disabilities (if present) sits and watches the other children at play.	The provider may believe that she is helping the child with disabilities by protecting him or her from potential frustration.	Through training and the loan of books, help the provider understand that children with disabilities thrive in inclusive environments.
Children who play with the same materials are expected to master the same learning goals at the same pace.	The provider might not understand that children progress through a series of developmental stages at their own paces and therefore take different amounts of time to learn new skills.	Reinforce for providers the concept that each child is unique, with an individual time clock for learning. Review Setting the Stage together.

Warning Signs	Why This Might Be Happening	What You Might Do
Very young children are habitually kept in high chairs, walkers, or playpens while older children play.	Most often, providers do this as an aid to managing children's behavior.	Explain to providers that while it's sometimes appropriate to put infants in these places (for instance, to allow them to participate in messy group activities without disturbing the other children), these should never become permanent resting places for children during the day. Children need to be free to explore their environment if they are to learn—not kept "prisoners" in playpens or high chairs.
Children watch educational television programming every day.	The provider might think that there are excellent programs on public television that can benefit children. Or the provider may think that there's no baby-sitter as good as TV.	Although there is some validity to the first statement, as a rule TV is not a substitute for good caregiving. With all the creative, innovative opportunities available for learning in a home, TV is a poor replacement for active learning. Work with the provider to develop alternative activities to TV-watching.

Specific Things To Look For

In addition to your general observations, you'll want to spend time observing how each of the nine separate activities are being implemented in a provider's home. There are, of course, a great many things that you should be looking for. We've included here what we consider to be some of the more important indicators of high-quality programming. Three examples are given for each activity. If a provider you're working with has not implemented all nine activities, you should naturally limit your observations to those indicators which relate to the activities actually being undertaken.

What You Should See	Why
Children use real props for dramatic play, such as dress-up clothes, old briefcases, jewelry, and so on.	The "realness" of props make dramatic play exciting to children. Adult props also give children a chance to make-believe they are acting like powerful people—their parents.
Children freely act out in their dramatic play otherwise "forbidden" activities such as giving a child a shot or hitting a baby.	Dramatic play enables children to deal with their emotions and problems in a risk-free environment. Hitting a doll lets children work through their anger in acceptable ways; giving another person a shot lets children work through their fear of doctors.

What You Should See	Why
Children try out a variety of roles, costumes, and props in their dramatic play.	Dramatic play lets children explore how different people live and act. It lets children combine the realities of everyday life with their own fantasies of what people are like.
Children experiment with blocks to build structures such as towers, bridges, and buildings.	Children need lots of first-hand experience before they learn about balance, weight, and directionality in building. Successful blockbuilding comes only when children have had lots of previous experiences in making towers that won't stand and buildings that easily collapse.
Children use props during block play.	Props can turn block play into dramatic play arenas: castles, rocket ships, and railroad yards can suddenly appear.
Providers use block-building time as opportunities to help children learn pre-math concepts such as classification, number, and proportion.	Unit blocks are an ideal teaching tool for introducing children to math concepts. Providers who introduce concepts such as "taller," "twice as big," "round" and "square" into their conversations with children can make good use of a natural learning opportunity.
Children use open-ended toys creatively without being encouraged by the provider to do it a particular or "right" way.	Open-ended materials allow children to solve problems and look at the world in different ways.
Children use a variety of toys together with other children, with the provider, and alone.	Children benefit from all these social configurations. They need time to try out many toys both alone and with others.
Children use household objects as "toys." For example, infants bang measuring spoons against a cup, or older children play with collections of bottle caps or fabric scraps.	A wide variety of toys does not require a large financial investment. Often, homemade or household toys are also the best because their familiarity invites children to play with them.
Children are encouraged during art play to be creative with materials, not to reproduce a designated model.	Asking children to recreate a model is both developmentally inappropriate and frustrating for children. Because art and creativity are natural partners, it makes better sense to emphasize this relationship.

What You Should See	**Why**
Children do a wide variety of art activities—not just drawing and painting.	Although drawing and painting are the cornerstones of children's art activities, there are many other activities, such as sculpting, weaving, making collages, and puppetry, which children also love. A balanced program ought to expose children to a variety of learning experiences.
The children's art work is displayed throughout the family child care home at the children's eye level.	Seeing their own work on display builds children's self-esteem as it gives them pride in their capabilities.
The provider reads to children of all ages.	Even preverbal infants can benefit from being read to. Nearly every child loves hearing a story and the closeness of being with the reader.
The provider asks questions as she reads a book to a child, such as "What do you think will happen next?" or "Why is the boy so sad?"	By questioning children, providers can help them better comprehend the story and relate it to their own lives.
Children look through books on their own.	Even if children can't yet read, the experience of looking at a book's pictures and turning pages teaches reading readiness. It also allows children to spend extra time alone with their favorite books.
The designated area for sand and water has been made safe (e.g., outlets covered, rubber slats placed on step ladders, play tubs in reach, etc.).	Safety must be a prerequisite for all play activities.
Children are allowed to be messy in their sand and water play.	Sand and water play go hand in hand with mud and mess. It is the freedom to be able to get dirty that makes this play so inviting to children. Careful preparation can reduce clean-up time.
Play props are made available to the children during sand and water play.	Measuring cups, sieves, colanders, and funnels can greatly enhance children's play.

What You Should See	Why
Cooking activities are tied into the day's routines (e.g., snack, lunch).	Letting children participate in preparing their own meals builds self-confidence. Most children take pride in being served a meal they have helped put together.
Nutrition information is interwoven into cooking activities. For example, children are told they need milk for lunch to make their bones and teeth strong and carrots at snack to help them see better.	Young children are very concerned about their growing bodies. Learning that what they eat affects their health can set the groundwork for a lifetime of healthy eating habits.
Children are encouraged to eat together "family-style."	Family-style dining is a time for sharing, caring, and responsibility. Family-style dining encourages interaction with all members of the family child care home, teaches self-help skills, and sets a relaxed tone for eating.
Children are encouraged to be creative with music.	Music allows children to explore their moods, to release their pent-up energy, and to feel good about themselves. Children need lots of opportunities to react freely to music. Music activities should be much more than playing an occasional record or tape together.
Music activities are spontaneous as well as planned.	To make music a part of children's lives, it should be ongoing and introduced informally as well as formally integrated into the curriculum.
Music and movement activities are used to help children control their moods and channel their energy appropriately.	Providers can help children make the transition into needed routines with effective background music. For instance, classical music played during quiet times can settle children down. Likewise, lively rock songs can be used for stretching activities to help children unwind.
An outdoor area, with spaces for practicing gross motor activities as well as quiet craft or play activities, is available to children.	The outdoor play area, like the indoor play area, should be organized to promote growth and learning. Children need space to run as well as quiet areas for examining plants or reading a book.

What You Should See	Why
Field trips are planned to supplement family child care activities.	Regular visits to the library plus occasional planned trips to a zoo, museum, farm, and so on can extend the curriculum beyond the family child care home and into the community.
Outdoor activities are scheduled twice daily except when the weather prohibits them.	All children benefit from being outdoors. Opportunities to stretch, run, and play with abandon are important to children's well-being. Fresh-air activities energize everyone.

When the Activities Are Inappropriate

If the activities being offered in a family child care home do not foster children's growth and development, you can focus your assistance on helping the provider plan activities that will be developmentally more appropriate. Here are some of the things you should look for as well as strategies to address potential problems.

Warning Signs	Why This Might Be Happening	What You Might Do
The provider intervenes when she sees a child hitting a doll or scolding a puppet.	The provider wants to help the child control his or her feelings in socially appropriate ways.	Review the activity unit on Dramatic Play with the provider, underscoring the need for children to have a play forum in which they can express their emotions freely.
The provider keeps young children from joining in dramatic play activities with the older children.	The provider doesn't want to ruin the older children's play time.	Help the provider develop strategies for including young children in play scenarios. Let her know that all children can benefit from dramatic play.
Only hardwood unit blocks are available for very young children to play with.	The provider believes unit blocks enhance her family child care program and has committed a large portion of her toy budget to their purchase.	Although this belief about blocks is true and should be commended, discuss with the provider the need for softer, lighter blocks for the younger children to play with. Using the activity unit on Blocks, show the provider how to make homemade blocks suitable for very young children.

Warning Signs	Why This Might Be Happening	What You Might Do
Children rarely have time to complete a block-building project before beginning clean-up.	The provider tries to adhere to the prearranged schedule for the day.	Discuss with the provider the need for occasionally extending times for block projects so that children can work at length on a big project. Also, encourage the provider to keep major creations on display for the day.
If a child has trouble doing a puzzle, the provider completes the puzzle for the child.	The provider might not want the child to become frustrated and quit trying.	Explain to the provider that children need time to explore and experiment with learning materials on their own. Children who are allowed the time to master puzzles or finish projects without adult assistance learn better than those who have their work done for them. If the puzzle is too developmentally advanced, the provider should offer the child a puzzle that is more in line with the child's developmental level.
Children always ask permission to use a new toy or to return one they are finished using.	The provider might think she is teaching children good manners by requiring them to request her permission.	Explain to the provider that children need free access to toys and materials to promote learning.
Young children are admonished by the provider for not using scissors or markers correctly.	The provider might feel that she or he is instructing the children in skills they need or might not realize that the children are not yet developmentally capable of the small motor control needed for using these implements.	Help the provider assess the children's capabilities in this area, explaining that many toddlers are not capable of using scissors or markers. Show the provider strategies for helping the children develop fine motor skills (for example, sifting sand, pouring juice) so that eventually they will be able to use scissors and markers.
The provider relies on dittos, coloring books, and pre-packaged art materials.	The provider might believe that materials developed by experts are better than the kinds of experiences she or he could devise.	Discuss with the provider how materials of this type thwart creativity. Hold a training session on making homemade art projects, as shown in the activity unit on Art.

Warning Signs	Why This Might Be Happening	What You Might Do
Only older children who know how to care for books are allowed to use them on their own.	The provider is trying to teach children to take care of their valuables.	Review the Books activity unit with the provider, stressing the need to let very young children explore books on their own. Suggest that the provider get some cloth or vinyl books for the infants and young toddlers to play with.
The provider uses books only as vehicles for teaching pre-reading skills.	The provider wants to make sure the children are well prepared for first-grade reading.	Although this is a commendable goal, help the provider view books as more than a precursor to reading readiness. Encourage the provider to make book times fun for children so that they will associate reading with pleasure.
Children have been warned of making a mess with sand and water; they spend only a few minutes at the play tubs.	The provider is overly concerned with maintaining order.	Review the Sand and Water activity unit with the provider, highlighting the need for children to be free to splash and poke if they are to enjoy their play.
Children have so many sand and water props to play with that they flit from prop to prop, doing little with any of them.	The provider is trying to extend the children's learning.	Caution the provider on the dangers of overstimulation. Work out a plan with the provider for gradually introducing props to children.
Children cannot reach counters and must strain to participate in cooking activities.	The provider has not recognized the need for accommodating the kitchen to the children's size.	Work with the provider to develop some alternative plans, such as bringing in child-sized tables as a work station.
Only older children are allowed in the kitchen for cooking activities.	The provider feels that the kitchen is too dangerous for young children.	Using the chapter on Cooking as a reference, develop some strategies for safely including young children in cooking activities—for example, kneading dough at a table or stirring batter in a bowl. Also, help the provider to childproof the kitchen so that safety will not be a constant concern.

Warning Signs	Why This Might Be Happening	What You Might Do
Only music from the provider's personal record collection or the radio are available for listening.	The provider believes that children can learn to enjoy the same music she or he does.	Although the provider should, of course, enjoy the music experiences, help her or him see the need for providing children with a rich variety of musical experiences.
The children play exclusively with store-bought, miniature musical instruments.	The provider takes pride in being able to buy high-quality toys for her children.	Using the chapter on Music and Movement as a reference, help the provider realize that real instruments–even homemade ones–provide more valuable learning experiences than "imitation" instruments.
Children run around outside without using toys and equipment or becoming involved in activities.	The provider might believe that it's healthy for children who have been "trapped" inside all day to let off steam.	Help the provider understand that while it is fine for children to run around, there comes a point when such behavior turns into chaos. Help the provider plan gross motor activities that will enable children to let loose. Suggest ideas for organizing the outdoor environment into interest areas (for example, a sand box with sifting and digging tools, a laundry tub filled with water and basters, a gardening spot, or an old tree trunk for carpentry).
Children look lost when taken on field trips, unsure of what they should be doing.	The provider has not prepared the children for the trip.	Using the Outdoors activity unit, review with the provider the need to consider field trips as an extension of the family child care curriculum. Help the provider plan pre- and post-field trip activities that will make field trips meaningful for the children.

Provider Interactions With Children

In observing how providers have incorporated the activities into their family child care program, you'll also want to take a look at how effectively they interact with children while doing these activities. To implement the program successfully, providers need to communicate positively and effectively with the children in their care. Here are some of the things you should be observing.

What You Should See	Why
The provider gives individual attention to each child (for example, a hug, a smile, rocking together in a rocking chair, or a pat on the head).	Warm nurturing is the backbone of family child care; all providers should naturally offer it.
The provider intervenes when one child hits another, bites another, or otherwise loses control.	Children need to learn that certain activities are not acceptable. By stepping in and gently but firmly restraining the out-of-control child, the provider lets all the children know what is and is not appropriate social behavior.
The provider tells a child when he or she is doing something against the rules (for example, shoving another child or spitting) but does not label the child "bad" or "nasty."	By letting children know that certain behaviors (for example, shoving, pulling hair, and spitting) are unacceptable, the provider assists children in establishing appropriate limits. At the same time, by criticizing the behavior and not the child, the provider does not hurt the child's self-esteem.
The provider encourages children to be independent. For example, during free play children select their own materials and are expected to clean up after themselves. Children also participate in preparing, serving, and cleaning up meals and snacks. The provider helps children master self-help boards and learn to dress themselves.	Children who are secure and confident learn to be independent and in control of their own lives. Learning to be self-sufficient is an important goal for all early childhood education.
The provider encourages children to share without demanding that children do this often before they are developmentally capable of doing so.	Sharing is a social skill important to growth and well-being. As appropriate, the provider can work on opportunities for children to play together, use the same art materials, and so on. The provider can also model appropriate sharing behavior as she or he eases children toward the attainment of this social skill.
The provider encourages children to develop self-control. For example, she or he helps children define appropriate limits, lets children know the rules of care, gives children positive encouragement for good behaviors, and doesn't threaten them.	Research shows that when discipline is intrinsically motivated (i.e., comes from within), it is more effective and lasting than discipline that is extrinsically motivated by threats and punishment.

When Interactions Are Inappropriate

Although you will probably observe many positive social interactions, not every provider will always be positive, nor will every home have an environment that fosters children's self-esteem. Here are some examples of warning signs that the interactions between provider and children are not appropriate.

Warning Signs	Why This Might Be Happening	What You Might Do
The provider excludes misbehaving children from popular activities such as blowing bubbles or going on a field trip.	The provider might believe that children will learn to behave appropriately if they are punished for their misbehavior.	Work with the provider to help her or him learn positive guidance techniques that promote self-control. Punishment such as this is too harsh for a young child.
The provider makes misbehaving children eat all their vegetables at lunch or deprives them of dessert.	The provider believes that food is an effective tool for managing children's behavior.	As before, work with the provider to develop a more appropriate approach to guidance. Also, conduct a workshop on why the use of food as reward or punishment teaches children the wrong messages about nutrition.
The provider reacts to a child's misbehavior without attempting to find out the cause of the child's actions.	The provider might not understand the concept that there are causes for children's misbehavior, and in order to help a child learn acceptable behaviors, adults must discover and address those causes.	Share with the provider the idea that misbehavior doesn't occur in a vacuum. Was the child testing limits? Does the child need extra attention because of something happening at home? Have the rules been communicated adequately to the child? Understanding the causes of misbehavior is a prerequisite to solving problem behaviors.
The provider lavishes children with compliments on how they look or dress.	The provider might be trying to build the children's self-confidence.	Discuss with the provider that although some compliments of this type are definitely in order, they should not be the only ones that children receive. Children need to feel valued for who they are—not what they look like.
The provider is inconsistent in disciplining, providing attention to, or working with children.	The provider might genuinely like some of the children in her or his care more than others.	Discuss with the provider the commitment to provide developmentally appropriate care to all children. Then help the provider learn to provide more even-handed caregiving. Also, point out how preferential, inconsistent caregiving affects all the children negatively.

Warning Signs	Why This Might Be Happening	What You Might Do
The provider talks to infants and toddlers in babytalk.	The provider might think that infants and toddlers will not understand "real" words.	Hold a workshop on the development of language in children. Model appropriate language for providers to use when talking to infants and toddlers while changing their diapers, putting them down for naps, or feeding them.
The provider leaves infants or toddlers in their cribs after they awaken, until whatever activity she or he is doing with the older children is over.	This is usually a management decision. The provider might have decided that it is easier for her to manage the group and avoid conflicts if the younger children are left in their cribs until it's convenient to get them.	Explain to the provider that children left unattended may become insecure. Help her or him plan the day so that waking children can be brought into a group event in a nondisruptive way.
The provider makes disparaging remarks about the children's parents to another adult in front of the children.	The provider might not think that the children can hear the negative remarks.	Parents are the most important people in young children's lives. For a provider to say negative things about these beloved ones is confusing and overwhelming to a young child. Discuss this with the provider and enlist her or his cooperation in this area.

In this chapter we've taken an in-depth look at how activities in *The Creative Curriculum for Family Child Care* are being used by providers. If you can help providers effectively implement these activities, you will begin to see developmentally appropriate care that meets the needs of all children in the program.

Appendix

Resources

I. Publications

A. Running a Family Child Care Home

American Academy of Pediatrics, American Public Health Association, & National Resource Center for Health and Safety in Child Care. (2002). *Caring for our children: National health and safety performance standards: Guidelines for out-of-home child care programs* (2nd ed.). Elk Grove Village, IL; Washington, DC; Aurora, CO: Author.

Alston, F. K. (1992). *Caring for other people's children: A complete guide to family day care* (Reissued and updated ed.). New York: Teachers College Press.

Bailey, R. A. (1997). *There's gotta be a better way: Discipline that works!* (Rev. ed.). Oviedo, FL: Loving Guidance.

Dodge, D. T., & Colker, L. J. (1991). *Caring and Learning* [Videotape]. Washington, DC: Teaching Strategies, Inc.

Gallagher, P. C. (1995). *Start your own at home child care business* (2nd ed.). Mosby.

Godwin, A., & Schrag, L. (1996). *Setting up for infant/toddler care: guidelines for centers and family child care homes* (Rev. ed.) Washington, DC: National Association for the Education of Young Children.

Gonzalez-Mena, J. (1991). *Tips and tidbits: A book for family day care providers*. Washington, DC: National Association for the Education of Young Children.

Levine, Karen. (2002). *A survival guide for child care providers: tips from the trenches*. Albany, NY: Delmar Thomson Learning.

Modigliani, K., Reiff, M., & Jones, S. (1987). *Opening your door to children: How to start a family day care program*. Washington, DC: National Association for the Education of Young Children.

National Association for the Education of Young Children. (n.d.). *The B.U.S.I.N.E.S.S. of Family Child Care*. [Videotape]. Washington, DC: Author.

National Association for Family Child Care. (1988, Fourth Rev. 1997). *Starting your own family child care business: Basic facts from the National Association For Family Child Care*. Salt Lake City, UT: Author. Retrieved June 11, 2003 from http://www.nafcc.org/starting.html

Pennsylvania AAP. (1999). *Preparing for illness: A joint responsibility for parents and caregivers* (Rev. ed.). Washington, DC: NAEYC; Elk Grove Village, IL: American Academy of Pediatrics.

B. Activities

Appleton, J., McCrea, N., & Patterson, C. (2001). *Do carrots make you see better? A guide to food and nutrition in early childhood programs.* Beltsville, MD: Gryphon House.

Bickart, T. S., & Dodge, D. T. (2000). *Reading right from the start: What parents can do in the first five years.* Washington, DC: Teaching Strategies, Inc.

Bowman, B. (Ed.). (2002). *Love to read: Essays in developing and enhancing early literacy skills of African American children.* Washington, DC: National Black Child Development Institute, Inc.

Dodge, D. T., Heroman, C., United States. Office of Educational Research and Improvement, & National Institute on Early Childhood Development and Education (U.S.) (1999). *Building your baby's brain: A parent's guide to the first five years.* Washington, DC: Teaching Strategies, Inc.

Kohl, M. F. (2000). *The big messy* art book: *But easy to clean up.* Beltsville, MD: Gryphon House.

Kohl, M. F. (2001). *Mudworks: Creative clay, dough and modeling experiences.* Beltsville, MD: Gryphon House.

Kohl, M. F., & Potter, J. (1997). *Cooking art: Easy edible art for young children.* Beltsville, MD: Gryphon House.

Ross, M. E. (1995). *Sandbox scientist: Real science activities for little kids.* Chicago, IL: Chicago Review Press.

Schickedanz, J. A. (1999). *Much more than the ABCs: The early stages of reading and writing.* Washington, DC: National Association for the Education of Young Children.

Zavitkovsky, A., Blakley, B., Brady, E., & Blau, R. (1989). *Activities for school-age child care.* Washington, DC: National Association for the Education of Young Children.

C. Feelings

Brazelton, T. B. (1992). *Touchpoints: Your child's emotional and behavioral development.* Reading, MA: Addison-Wesley.

Greenspan, S. I., & Greenspan, N. T. (1985). *First feelings: Milestones in the emotional development of your baby and child.* New York: Penguin Books.

Greenspan, S. I., & Wieder, S. (1998). *The child with special needs: Encouraging intellectual and emotional growth.* Cambridge, MA: Perseus Publishing.

Lieberman, A.F. (1993). *The emotional life of the toddler.* New York: Free Press.

D. Multicultural Resources

A.B.C. Task Force, & Derman-Sparks, Louise. (1989). *Anti-bias curriculum: Tools for empowering young children.* Washington, DC: National Association for the Education of Young Children.

Bisson, J. (1997). *Celebrate! An anti-bias guide to enjoying holidays in early childhood programs.* Saint Paul, MN: Redleaf Press.

Schniedewind, N., & Davidson, E. (1998). *Open minds to equality: A sourcebook of learning activities to affirm diversity and promote equality* (2nd ed.). Boston, MA: Allyn & Bacon.

II. Publishers/Information Sources: An Introductory List

Gryphon House, Inc.
www.ghbooks.com
P.O. Box 207
Beltsville, MD USA 20704
301-595-9500
800-638-0928 (orders, US only)
Fax: 301-595-0051

Redleaf National Institute ("the national
center for the business of family child care")
www.redleafinstitute.org
450 North Syndicate, Suite 5
St. Paul, MN 55104
651-641-6675
Fax: 800-641-0115

Redleaf Press
www.redleafpress.org
450 North Syndicate, Suite 5
Saint Paul, Minnesota 55104
800-423-8309
Fax: 800-641-0115

Teaching Strategies, Inc.
www.TeachingStrategies.com
P.O. Box 42243
Washington, DC 20015
800-637-3652
Fax: 202-374-7273

Professional Organizations

Association for Childhood Education
International (ACEI)
www.udel.edu/bateman/acei
17904 Georgia Avenue, Suite 215
Olney, MD 20832
800-423-3563

The Children's Foundation
www.childrensfoundation.net
725 Fifteenth Street NW, Suite 505
Washington, DC 20005-2109
202-347-3300
Fax: 202-347-3382

Children's Defense Fund
www.childrensdefense.org
25 E Street, NW
Washington, DC 20001
202-628-8787 or 800-233-1200

Council for Professional Recognition
www.cdacouncil.org
2460 16th Street, NW
Washington DC 20009-3575
202-265-9090 or 800-424-4310
Fax: 202-265-9161

National Association for the Education of Young
Children (NAEYC)
www.naeyc.org
1509 16th Street, NW
Washington, DC 20036
800-424-2460

National Association for Family Child Care
http://www.nafcc.org
5202 Pinemont Drive
Salt Lake City, Utah 84123
801-269-9338
Fax: 801-268-9507

National Child Care Information Center
www.nccic.org
243 Church Street, NW, 2nd Floor
Vienna, VA 22180
800-616-2242
Fax: 800-716-2242
TTY: 800-516-2242

National Black Child Development Institute
www.nbcdi.org
1101 15th Street, NW, Suite 900
Washington, DC 20005
202-833-2220
Fax: 202-833-8222